Spanish Baby Names

Books by Judy Sierra

Celtic Baby Names
Cinderella
Nursery Tales Around the World
Quests and Spells
Storytellers' Research Guide

with Bob Kaminski

Multicultural Folktales
Twice Upon a Time
Children's Traditional Games

SPANISH BABY NAMES

Traditional and Modern First Names
of Spain and the Americas

Judy Sierra

FOLKPRINT

FOLKPRINT
77 Monte Cresta Avenue
Oakland CA 94611
folkprint@earthlink.net

Manufactured in the United States of America

Cover art: Elisa Kleven.
Cover design: Lyle Mayer.

Library of Congress Cataloging-in-Publication Data:

Sierra, Judy.
Spanish baby names : traditional and modern first names of
Spain and the Americas / Judy Sierra.
        p.   cm.
Includes bibliographical references (p.)
    ISBN 0-9636089-6-7 (paper)

1. Names, Personal–Spanish. 2 Names, Personal–Dictionaries.
3. Names, Personal–Spain. 4. Names, Personal–Latin America.
I. Title.

CS2377.S49   2002   929'.4'4'0946–dc21   2001006001

Spanish Baby Names

Mothers and fathers in Spanish-speaking countries express their family and religious identities through baby names, bestowing upon children the names of relatives, ancestors, saints and holy persons. Often, they reach beyond these traditions to create new names for new family members, or they may choose the name of a famous person, an interesting fictional character, a nature word or a spiritual concept.

In many families, baby naming follows an established order. The first son may receive his father's father's name, the second son his mother's father's name. Likewise, girls are named for their grandmothers. After grandparents' names, those of parents, aunts, uncles, and more distant relations are called into service. In this way, families pass along first names like heirlooms from generation to generation. Babies may also be named for godparents, family friends, and local and national heroes and heroines. The tradition of giving children the names of Christian saints began in the 4th century. Later, the Roman Catholic Church would insist that parents choose saints' names and Bible names as baptismal names. Jesús and María and the saints, with their exceptional powers, were expected to watch over and protect their namesakes. Each year, saints are remembered on feast days—the anniversaries of their ascent to heaven. Parents often give a newborn the name of a saint whose feast day falls on or near the date of the child's birth or baptism, or of a saint to whom they have a particular devotion.

The Spanish custom of giving a child two, three or more first names allows parents to follow several naming traditions at once. It also provides children with a choice of names to use later in their lives.

A brief history of Spanish names

In the centuries before the birth of Christ, the people who lived in the region that is now Spain spoke a variety of languages including Celtiberian (a relative of Irish and Welsh), Phoenician, Latin and Greek. By 19 BC, the Iberian Peninsula had become part of the Roman Empire with Latin as its official language. Although most ancient people were known by a single name, a Roman used a first name plus two or three family and clan names. As the Romans and their subjects converted to Christianity, they created new names from Latin words that expressed their faith, names like Amadeo, which means "love to God'. They also named their children for Christian holy days such as the Epiphany (which became Epifanio and Epifania in modern Spanish) and Christmas (Natalio and Natalia) and for religious concepts like resurrection (Anastasia and Anastasio).

In 400 AD, the Visigoths, a Germanic tribe from the north, took control of the Iberian Peninsula. The Visigoths soon began to speak the local language—a form of Latin that was evolving into Spanish. For some reason, though, their subjects quickly adopted the names of the Visigoth conquerors. Some scholars believe that this happened because the people of Spain disliked their former Roman overlords so much that they were happy to be rid of them *and* their names. The Visigoths' Germanic names were made up of two name-elements—words related to power, battles, weapons, gods and sacred animals. Modern Spanish names of Visigoth origin include Federico from *fridu* 'peace' + *ric* 'king', Rosamunda from *hros* 'horse' + *mund* 'protector', and Raúl from *rad* 'counsel, advice' + *wulf* 'wolf'. Although we know the meanings of individual name-elements, the relationship between pairs is not always understood.

After the Visigoths' dominance ended in 711 AD, their names inexplicably became even more popular in Spain than before, particularly among the nobility. Because so many Spanish conquerors and settlers of the New World came from the upper classes (nobles down on their luck, and the younger sons of wealthy families), Visigoth names have been especially widespread and enduring in the Americas. Of the names of Muslims who dominated the Iberian Peninsula in the Middle Ages, only a handful remained after 1492. Muslims and Jews were banished from Spain in that year, and a royal decree forbade the use of their names. Most traditional Spanish names of Hebrew origin, such as Arón and David, are not legacies of the Spain's once-flourishing Jewish population, but names chosen from the Bible by Christian parents.

Last names, or surnames, which are passed along unchanged from parent to child, became common in Western Europe in medieval times. Some of these surnames describe a person's profession or accomplishments, like the Spanish Herrera, which meant 'a smith', or Romero, which was originally a name for someone who had made a pilgrimage to Rome. Nobles took the names of their hereditary land. Many last names were patronymics formed by adding -ez or -iz or -es to the father's first name. At first, patronymics changed with each generation, but eventually they became permanent last names. Some popular medieval first names that are now out of fashion—Nuño, Vasco and Lope, for example—survive as last names—Nuñez, Vasquez and Lopez.

Near the end of the Middle Ages, in Spain and across Europe, the name stock (the total number of first names in use) declined rapidly. A survey of first names in one region of Spain reveals that in the year 1000, about 70 different names were used for each 100 people. By 1200, there were only 12 to 15 names per hundred people. Still, a new crop of first names did appear in Spain during the Middle Ages and Renaissance. For the first time, newly canonized saints had last names. Because there were already so many saints named Victor, José, and so on, parents began to convert the family names of the new saints into first names. San José Oriol inspired the boys' name, Oriol. Boys were named Borja and girls were named Borjita in honor of San Francisco de Borja y Aragón. The names Belarmino and Belarmina honored the Italian saint, Roberto Belarmino. Saints from faraway places brought names from other languages into the Spanish name stock, such as the Czech Wenceslao, Polish Casimiro and English Eduardo. Popular literature inspired parents to give their sons the names of the brave knights Rolando and Olivero, and their daughters those of the heroines Aldonza and Oliana. Fictional characters created by Cervantes, Shakespeare, Chaucer, Bocaccio and other writers inspired new Spanish names.

Before the year 800, few parents named their daughters María. The name was considered too holy. This attitude changed over the course of the Middle Ages so that by 1600, María had attained overwhelming popularity, giving rise to dozens of related names like Dolores, Carmen, Consuelo, Paz, Remedios and Socorro. Some of these names refer to invocations of the Virgin, for example, Consuelo for Nuestra Señora del Divino Consuelo (Our Lady of Divine Consolation) and Paz for Nuestra Señora de la Paz (Our Lady of Peace). Other names honor sites of Marian apparitions, such as Guadalupe in Mexico and Lourdes in France, or places where ancient madonna statues were found, like Montserrat in the Catalan region of Spain. Many of these Marian names were originally second names added to María, such as Carmen from María del Carmen.

The meanings of names

Peoples' names began as words everyone understood, but over the centuries names and everyday vocabulary evolved and changed in different ways. By 900 AD, scholars were merely guessing at the meanings of names, and usually guessing wrong. Today, advances in linguistics and genealogy have made it possible for researchers to be fairly certain of the origin and meaning of most Spanish first names. In some cases, though, we may know the dictionary meaning of a name, yet not entirely understand what the name meant to the people who chose it. The meanings of some names are not yet known, while those of others are disputed.

In ancient times, children were given the names gods and goddesses: Dionisio is from the name of the Greek god Dionysios, for example, and Flora was a Roman goddess of flowers and springtime. Some early names were words for animals: Úrsula comes from a Latin word for 'little bear'; Rodolfo meant 'glorious wolf' in the Germanic language of the Visigoths. Animal names like these probably had sacred meanings. Parents expressed their hopes for their children by giving them good-luck names like Fausto, Feliciano and Fortunato, all from Latin words meaning 'lucky'. Many names expressed gratitude to gods and goddesses for a child's birth, for instance, Samuel, from the Hebrew 'God has listened [to a prayer for a child]' and Isidoro, from ancient Greek 'gift of the goddess Isis'.

More down-to-earth first names told of a person's place of origin, like Hadrianus (modern Spanish Adrián and Adriana), a Latin name for a person from the city of Hadria in northern Italy. Some Roman names describe the circumstances of a baby's birth: Agripino comes from a Latin word meaning 'born feet-first', and numerical names like Quinto and Quinta ('fifth') indicate a baby's birth order in the family. Some glorious and famous Roman names began as nicknames that might seem rather unkind, for example, Claudius (Spanish Claudio), which meant a person who walked with a limp, and Cicero (Cicerón) 'garbanzo bean', a nickname for a person with warts. Regardless of their origin and meaning, nearly every ancient name that has endured as a Spanish baby name was at some time the name of a Christian saint.

Saints' names and feast days

When choosing baby names, Roman Catholic parents may consult calendars of saints' feast days, known as *santorals* in Spanish. Surprisingly, the date given for a particular name often varies from one calendar to another. This is because so many saints have shared the same names. There have been more than 500 San Juans! One saint may be recognized in the santoral of a particular church, another saint by the same name in the santoral of another, each with a different feast day. Over the years, saints have come and gone from these official lists. Important figures from the Old Testament and even the archangels have been proclaimed preChristian saints with their own feast days. In the following list of baby names, dates are given only for major saints whose feast days are standard in all Roman Catholic countries, and for prominent saints from Spanish-speaking areas. Lives of the saints may be found on the web sites listed in the bibliography on page 107. Santorals for specific regions can be found by performing an Internet search for the name of a country or city along with the word 'santoral'.

Boys' names and girls' names

The custom of giving boys and girls slightly different forms of the same name began in ancient Rome, where girls bore feminine versions of their fathers' names, and a woman named Julia was probably the daughter of a man named Julius (her sister was probably named Julia, too). Spanish pairs are formed in a similar way, with -*o* usually replacing the Latin masculine -*us*. Although in the Roman system women's names were based men's names, Spanish men's names were often created from women's names. Cecilio and Catalino, for example, are men's names bestowed in honor of the female saints Cecilia and Catalina. A few religious names, like Reyes, Guadalupe and Trinidad can be given to either a boy or a girl. María is used as a man's middle name, as is Jesús or de Jesús for women.

Many more girls than boys receive nontraditional names. This is true not only in Spanish-speaking countries, but throughout Europe and the Americas. There have been international fads and trends in girls' names such as flower names and precious stone names in the late 19th and early 20th centuries. Girls are also more likely than boys to receive the names of fictional characters and names from other languages.

The Spanish custom of blending two girls' names into one produced Alondra, a blend of Alicia and Sondra; Anatilde, a blend of Ana and Matilde, and other delightful names. In fact, there are so many blends and variants of Spanish girls' names that it can be difficult to know how a particular name evolved. Malena, for example, is a blend of María and Elena. It is also a diminutive of Magdalena, and in South America it is a variant form of Malén, a native name from the Mapuche language.

Familiar forms of names

Diminutives are the special forms of names used by a person's family and friends. The usual way of forming a diminutive in Spanish is by adding -ita or -cita to a girl's name, -ito, -cito or -illo to a boy's name, after dropping any final vowels. In this book, common forms of diminutives are given only if they are not formed in a usual way. Diminutives can also be created by shortening a name. A remarkable number of diminutives in all languages mimic the way young children mispronounce a name: Tata for Altagracia, for example, and Lalo for Eduardo. Diminutives sometimes become official first names. Anita, once a diminutive of Ana, is now a baptismal name with its own diminutive, Nita. Although some Spanish feminine diminutives are formed by adding -ina or -iana, most names ending in -ino, -ina, -iano and -iana are not diminutives. They are derived from Roman family and clan names. For example, the names Maximinus and Maximianus (which became Maximino and Maximiano in modern Spanish) once signified that a person belonged to the family or clan of a man named Maximus.

Names in minority languages

Until 1977, the government of Spain required that all children's names be in the official language, Castilian Spanish. First names in Spain's minority languages could not be registered. Governments of other Spanish-speaking countries had similarly restrictive laws. Most of these laws were repealed in the latter part of the 20th century, and today the minority language names of Spain and the native names of Latin America are experiencing a lively revival. Names in the Romance languages of Catalan, Galician and Asturian are fairly similar in spelling and pronunciation to those of Castilian Spanish. The Basque language is not related to Spanish, or to any other language, for that matter. Linguists speculate that it may be the oldest language in Europe. Few ancient Basque names have survived, though, and most in use today are Basque spellings of Spanish and French first names, Basque vocabulary words, or place names like Arantxa, for the site of an apparition of the Virgin Mary. This book includes a selection of Basque, Catalan and Galician names, along with some popular indigenous names from Latin America. More complete sources of names in these languages are listed in the bibliography on page 107.

The spelling of Spanish names

Spanish first names often have several different accepted spellings, especially in the Americas. If you have difficulty locating a particular name in this book, try making substitutions based on these common changes:

The letters *b* and *v* are interchangeable in some names;

h, because it is silent, may have been dropped from the beginning of a name;

c, s and *z* are interchangeable in some positions, including the beginnings of names;

j and *x* sound alike, and may be interchangeable;

some pairs of vowels are interchangeable, either because they sound somewhat alike, or because, at some point in history they looked alike when handwritten: *i* and *e, a* and *o, a* and *u,* and *o* and *u,* are the most frequent substitutions, however, any vowel substitution is possible.

Recently, parents have begun spelling traditional names in creative ways. Often, they use letters and letter combinations that do not occur in Spanish, such as *k, ck,* double letters, and *-i, -ie* and *-y* endings. An example of this creative spelling is Kasey, used as a name in its own right and as a diminutive of Casandra.

Pronunciation Guide

In words ending with vowels, *-n* or *–s,* syllable stress is on the next-to-last syllable. Stress in other words is on the last syllable. An accent over a vowel overrides these two rules and places stress on that syllable. Spanish contains three letters not found in English: *ch, ll* and *ñ*. In Spanish dictionaries, *ch* comes after *c, ll* after *l,* and *ñ* after *n*. In this book, however, names are alphabetized in English dictionary order.

Spanish	English sound is like
a	*a* in f*a*ther
ai	*ie* in t*ie*
au	*ou* in *ou*t
b	*b* in *b*oy
c	*c* in *c*at, or before e or i, like th in *th*in (Castilian) or like *s* in *s*it
ch	*ch* in *ch*ip
d	*d* in *d*og
e	*ai* in *ai*r (short, not 'ay-eee')
ei	*ay* in s*ay*
f	*f* in *f*un
g	*g* in *g*ate, or, before e or i, like *ch* in Scottish lo*ch*.
h	is silent
i	*ee* in n*ee*d
ie	*ye* in *ye*t
j	*h* in *h*ot or like *ch* in Scottish lo*ch*.

k	*k* in *k*iss
l	*l* in *l*et
ll	*lli* in mi*lli*on
m	*m* in *m*eet
n	*n* in *n*ice
ñ	*ni* in onion or *ny* in canyon
o	*o* in n*o*te
oi, oy	*oy* in r*oy*al
p	*p* in *p*at
qu	*k* in *k*iss
r, rr	trilled, by tapping the tip of the tongue just behind the top front teeth. Double r is trilled several times.
s	*s* in *s*oap
t	*t* in *t*on
u	*oo* in b*oo*t; silent in gue, gui, que, qui.
ua	*ua* in q*ua*lity
v	*b* in *b*oy
w	*v* in *v*ery.
x	In names, like *h* in *h*ot.
y	as a vowel, like *ee* in n*ee*d; as a consonant, like *y* in *y*es
z	*s* in *s*oap; in Castilian, like *th* in *th*in.

Aarón, Arón Hebrew for 'exalted one'. In the Bible, Aaron was the first high priest of the Israelites. Feminine: Arona. English: Aaron.

Abel, Abé Hebrew 'Breath, vapor'. In the Bible, Abel was the younger son of Adam and Eve. English: Abel.

Abelardo A hybrid of the Hebrew name Abel and the Germanic name-element, *hard* 'strong, brave'. Diminutives: Abel, Beluch, Lalo.

Abelino, Avelino From Aveline, a medieval French women's name, diminutive of Latin *avis* 'bird'. Dim: Lino. Fem: Abelina, Avelina.

Abilio, Abil Latin *habilis* 'skilled, expert'. Fem: Abila, Abilia.

Abraham, Abrám, Abrán Hebrew for 'father of a multitude'. Abraham is considered a patriarch, or forefather, in the Jewish, Christian and Islamic religions. Dim: Brancho. English: Abraham. See also Ibrán.

Absalón 'Father of peace' in Hebrew. In the Bible, Absalom was the third son of King David.

Abundio Latin *abundans* 'abundant'. A popular name among early Christians. It signified the spiritual abundance they found in their new faith. San Abundio was a bishop of Córdoba, Spain, in the 9th century. Feast July 11. Dim: Abundi.

Acacio Greek *akakia* 'innocence'. Dim: Acaz. Fem: Acacia.

Acisclo Latin *acisculus,* a tool used for sharpening stones. San Acisclo, a 4th century Spanish martyr, is patron saint of Córdoba, Spain. Feast November 17. Catalan: Iscle.

Adalberto, Adelberto, Edilberto Germanic *adal* 'noble' + *berht* 'shining, brilliant'. Dims: Adal, Berto, Beto.

Adán, Adamo Hebrew for 'earth'. English: Adam.

Adauto, Adauco Latin *adauctus* 'large, full'.

Adelberto see Adalberto

Adelfo Greek *adelphos* 'brother'. Dim: Fito. Fem: Adelfa.

Adelgundis, Aldegundo, Aldegundis Germanic *adal* 'noble' + *gundi* 'war'. Fem: Adelgunda.

Adelio, Adelo, Adelino Germanic *adal* 'noble'. Dim: Lino. Fem: Adela, Adelia, Adelina.

Adelmaro Edelmaro Germanic *adal* 'noble' + *mar* 'fame'. Diminutives: Delmar, Demario, Delmario, Delmaro. Fem: Delmira, Dalmira, Edelmira.

Adelmo Germanic *adal* 'noble' + *helm* 'protector'. Dim: Delmo. Fem: Adelma.

Adilón Germanic *adal* 'noble'.

Adolfo Germanic *adal* 'noble' + *wulf* 'wolf'. Dims: Dolfito, Dolfo, Fito. Fem: Adolfina. English: Adolph.

Adonías Hebrew 'God is Lord'.

Adonis, Adón From the Semitic *adon* 'master, man'. A name from Greek myth. The god Adonis was renowned for his youth and beauty.

Adrián, Adriano, Adrión Latin Hadrianus, a name for a native of Hadria, a city in northern Italian on the Adriatic Sea. The name of six popes. Dim: Adri. Catalan: Adrià. Basque: Adiran. Fem: Adriana. English: Adrian.

Adriel Hebrew 'one of God's flock'.

Afraín see Efraín.

Africano From the Roman name Africanus 'a native of Africa', derived from Arabic *afar* 'dust'. Fem: Africa.

Agapito, Agapio Greek *agape* 'love'. A popular name in early Christian times. When the Romans threw San Agapito to the lions, the lions miraculously refused to eat him. Feast August 18. Dim: Pito. Fem: Agapita.

Agenor Greek *agathos* 'good' + *aner* 'man'. The name of a warrior in the ancient Greek epic, the *Iliad*.

Agosto, Agusto see Augusto.

Agripino From the Roman clan name Agrippinus 'a relative of Agrippa', derived from Latin *agrippa*, which means 'born feet first'. One of the most illustrious Roman family names. Dims: Agripí, Pino. Fem: Agripina.

Aguinaldo Germanic *agin* 'blade' + *wald* 'ruler, governor'. This name is used in the Philippines to honor the independence leader Emilio Aguinaldo (1869-1964). Dims: Nayo, Naldo.

Agustín, Augustín From a Roman clan name, Augustinus 'a relative of Augustus', from Latin *augustus* 'magnificent, dignified'. San Agustín (Saint Augustine) is the patron saint of printers and theologians. Feast August 28. Dims: Tin, Tino. Basque: Auxtina. Fem: Agustina.

Agusto see Augusto

Ahuízotl Nahuatl 'otter'. The name of an Aztec chief of Tenochtitlan.

Aitor Basque *aita* 'father', a name given in honor of the legendary forefather of the Basque people. The name itself is a literary creation of the 19th century writer Agustín Chao.

Alamán see Almano

Alamar, Alamiro see Alomar

Alán, Alano From the name of a tribe, the Alans, originally from Asia Minor, who were driven into Spain by the Huns in the 4th century. Another possible etymology is Celtic *ail* 'noble'. Fem: Alana. English: Alan.

Alarico Germanic *al* 'all' + *ric* 'king'. The name of the Visigoth chief who sacked Rome in 400 AD. Dim: Rico.

Albán, Albano Latin Albanus, a name for a native of any one of several Roman cities named Alba (Latin for 'white'). Fem: Albana.

Albertín, Albertino A hybrid name from the Germanic *adal* 'noble' + *berht* 'shining, brilliant', with a Latin ending. Dim: Tino. Fem: Albertina.

Alberto, Aliberto, Oberto Germanic *adal* 'noble' + *berht* 'shining, brilliant'.

Originally a contraction of the name Adalberto. San Alberto, a 13th century priest and scientist, is remembered on November 15. Dims: Berto, Beto, Veto. Catalan: Albert. Fem: Alberta. English: Albert.

Albino, Albiano From Albinus, a Roman family name, derived from Latin *albus* 'white'. Diminutive: Bino. Fem: Albina.

Alceo Greek *alke* 'strength', an epithet of Hercules.

Aldegundis see Adelgundis

Aldemar, Aldemaro Germanic *ald* 'old, venerable' + *mar* 'fame'.

Aldo, Aldino, Aldano Germanic *ald* old, venerable' or *adal* 'noble' (sounds of the letters *d* and *l* were sometimes reversed in Spanish names). Fem: Alda, Aldana.

Aldonso, Aldonzo Masculine forms of Aldonza, a name invented and made popular by the Spanish writer Miguel de Cervantes.

Alegre 'Happy, joyful' in Spanish. Fem: Alegra.

Aleix Catalan form of Alejo.

Alejandrino, Alejandrín A hybrid name, from Greek *alexein* 'defender' + *andros* 'of man', with a Latin ending. Dims: Drino, Sandrino.

Alejandro, Alesandro, Alexandro Greek *alexein* 'defender' + *andros* 'of man'. There were many early Christian saints by this name, but its popularity is mostly due to admiration for Alexander the Great, inspired by medieval romances. Dims: Al, Aleco, Aleix, Alex, Aljo, Jando, Jandro, Jano, Lejandro, Llejandro, Sandro. Fem:

Alejandra, Alesandra, Alessandra. Catalan: Alexandre, Aleixandre. Basque: Alesander. English: Alexander.

Alejo, Alexis Greek *alexein* 'defender'. Catalan: Aleix. Fem: Alicia. English: Alec, Alex.

Alepio, Alepo see Alipio

Alexis see Alejo

Alfeo, Alfio From *Alpha*, the first letter of the Greek alphabet. An early Christian name, referring to God as the Alpha and the Omega, the beginning and the end. Fem: Alfa, Alfia.

Alfonsino A hybrid name from Germanic *al* 'all' + *funs* 'ready', with a Latin ending. Fem: Alfonsina.

Alfonso, Alfonzo Germanic *al* 'all' + *funs* 'ready'. A Spanish royal name, borne by several kings of Asturia and León. San Alfonso is the patron saint of Mallorca. Dims: Alf, Alfie, Alfo, Foncho, Fonso, Poncho. Fem: Alfonsa. English: Alphonse.

Alfredo, Alfred Germanic *alf* 'an elf, a supernatural being' + *rad* 'advice, counsel'. Dims: Alfi, Fito, Feyo, Fredo. Fem: Alfreda. Catalan: Alfred. Basque: Alperda. English: Alfred.

Aliberto see Alberto

Alicio Masculine form of Alicia, from Aliz, a French diminutive of Adelaide.

Alipio, Alepio, Alepo Greek *alipes* 'without sadness'.

Almano, Alamán Germanic *adal* 'noble' + *man* 'man'.

Almaquio, Almaquino Greek *allos* 'foreign' + *machos* 'combat'. San Almaquio, a Roman martyr, opposed gladiatorial sports. Feast January 1. Fem: Almaquina.

Aloisio From Provençal Aloys, a name which has the same source as Luis: *hlod* 'glory' + *wig* 'combat'. Sixteenth century Italian saint Aloysius Gonzaga is patron of Catholic young people. Feast June 21. English: Aloysius.

Alomar, Alamar, Alamiro Germanic *ald* 'old, venerable' + *mar* 'fame'.

Alonso A name from the same source as Alfonso: Germanic *al* 'all' + *funs* 'prepared'. Dim: Lonso. Fem: Alonsa. English: Alonzo.

Álvar, Álvaro, Álvarez Germanic *adal* 'noble' + *ward* 'guardian'. This was a very popular name during the Middle Ages. San Álvaro established a Dominican center of learning in Spain in the 14th century. Feast February 19. Dims: Alvi, Lalo, Varo. Catalan: Alvar. Basque: Albar. Fem: Álvara.

Alvino Germanic *alf* 'elf, supernatural being' or *adal* 'noble' + *win* 'friend'. English: Alvin.

Amabilio, Amable Latin *amabilis* 'amiable, lovable'.

Amadeo Latin *amare* 'love' + *Deum* 'to God'. A name created by early Christians. Dim: Cheo. Fem: Amadea.

Amadís The Spanish version of an Old French name, Amadis, from Latin *amatus* 'loved'. This name derived its popularity from the hero of *Amadís de Gaula,* a medieval Spanish romance of chivalry. Fem: Amadisa.

Amado Latin *amatus* 'beloved'. Fem: Amada, Amata.

Amador Latin *amator* 'friend, one who loves'. Dim: Amor.

Amalarico see Manrique

Amalio Germanic *amal* 'work'. Fem: Amalia.

Amancio Latin *amans* 'loving'. Diminutive: Mancho. Fem: Amancia.

Amando, Amante Latin *amando* 'loving'. San Amando, who lived in the 7th century, is patron saint of winemakers. Feast February 6. Dim: Mando. Fem: Amanda.

Amaranto Greek *amaranto* 'imperishable'. Dim: Amario. Fem: Amaranta.

Amaru The name of a sacred serpent in Quechua, language of the Inca Empire.

Ambrosio Greek *ambrosios* 'immortal'. San Ambrosio (Saint Ambrose), a 4th century bishop of Milan, is patron saint of beekeepers and candlemakers. Feast December 7. Fem: Ambrosia. English: Ambrose.

Amelio From Aemilius, a Roman clan name derived from Latin *aemulus* 'rival'. Dim: Mel. Fem: Amelia.

Américo Germanic *haim* 'home' + *ric* 'king'. Spanish form of the Italian name Amerigo, a cognate of the Spanish name, Enrique. Dim: Merco. Fem: América.

Amílcar Phonecian *hi* 'friend' + Melkar, a Tyrian god. Amílcar (Hamilcar in English) was a Carthaginian general who attacked the Roman Empire in the 3rd century BC. He founded a settlement that became the city of Barcelona.

Amintor Greek *amynos* 'defender'. Fem: Aminda, Aminta.

Amor see Amador

Amós Hebrew 'borne by God'. A prophet and a book of the Old Testament. English: Amos.

Anacleto From Greek *anakletos* 'asked for help'. The name of the 3rd pope. Dim: Cleto.

Anastasio Greek *anastasis* 'resurrection'. Dims: Anastas, Nacho, Tacho, Tasio. Fem: Anastasia.

Anatolio Greek *anatole* 'dawn, east'. Dim: Antolín.

Ander Basque form of Andrés.

Andoni Basque form of Antonio.

Andoquino, Andoquio Greek *andokeo* 'incomparable'.

Andrés, Andreo Greek *andreios* 'manly, brave'. Saint Andrew was the first disciple of Jesus. Feast November 30. Dims: Andi, Andy. Basque: Ander. Catalan: Andreu. Fem: Andrea, Andresa. English: Andrew.

Andros A diminutive of Leandro.

Ángel, Angelo, Angelino Greek *angelos,* a word which meant 'messenger' in classical times and later 'angel' in Christian times. Dims: Gelito, Gelo, Lito. Catalan: Angel. Basque: Gotzon. Fem: Ángela. English: Angel, Angelo.

Aniano Latin *agnus* 'lamb'. Feminine: Aniana.

Aníbal Phonecian *hann* 'grace' + *Baal,* a deity. The name of the Carthaginian general (Hannibal in English) who invaded Rome by way of Spain in the 3rd century BC.

Aniceto Greek *aniketos* 'invincible'. Dim: Cheto.

Anselmo Germanic *Ans,* the name of a god + *helm* 'protector'. Dims: Chelmo, Chemo. Fem: Anselma. English: Anselm.

Antelmo The Italian cognate of Anselmo and the name of a 12th century Italian saint who was Archbishop of Canterbury, England. Feast June 26.

Antemio A name of Germanic origin, equivalent of Anselmo. Dim: Chemo.

Antéo Greek *anteos* 'opponent'. Fem: Antéa.

Antero, Antés Greek *antheros* 'heavenly'. The name of an ancient Greek god of passion and tenderness, and of a 3rd century pope.

Antimo, Antimio Greek *anthimos* 'flowery'. Fem: Antía.

Antolín see Anatolio. Dim: Lin.

Antoni Catalan form of Antonio.

Antoniano From the Latin name Antonianus 'a relative of Antonius'. Dim: Tonio. Fem: Antoniana.

Antonino From a Latin name, Antoninus 'a relative of Antonius'. Dims: Tonio, Toñin. Fem: Antonina.

Antonio, Antón From Antonius, a Roman clan name of Etruscan origin. The meaning of the name is not known. San Antonio (Saint Anthony of Egypt, 251-356) founded the first Christian monastery. Feast January 17. Another San Antonio, of Padua, Italy (1195-1231) is the patron saint of Portugal and of travelers. Feast June 13. Dims: Nico, Toni, Tonio, Toño, Tony. Catalan: Antoni. Basque: Andoni, Antton. Fem: Antonia. English: Anthony.

Aparicio Latin *apparitio* 'to wait on, to serve'. An early Christian name.

Apolinar, Apolinario Latin *apollinarus* 'sacred to Apollo', Roman god of archery, poetry, prophecy and the sun. Dims: Poli, Polín. Fem: Apolinaria.

Apolo, Apolón, Apolonio From Latin Apollo, the Roman god of archery, poetry, prophecy and the sun. Dim: Polo.

Aquileo, Aquilo, Aquilón From the Roman family name Aquilius, derived from Latin *aquilo* 'north wind'. In the Bible, the name of a tentmaker who welcomed Saint Paul. Dims: Lino, Loño, Quilo. Fem: Aquilina.

Aquiles From Greek Achilleus, one of the heroes of Homer's *Iliad*. The meaning of the name is unknown. Dim: Quilo. English: Achilles.

Arcadio Greek Arkadios, a name for a native of the Greek province of Arcadia, legendary home of Arcas, the son of Zeus. Dim: Cadio. Fem: Arcadia.

Arcángel Spanish for 'archangel'. Fem: Arcángela.

Archibaldo, Arquibaldo Germanic *ercan* 'natural, genuine' + *bald* 'daring, bold'. Dim: Baldo. English: Archibald.

Argentino, Argento Spanish *argento* 'silver'. Dim: Tino. Fem: Argentina, Argenta.

Arián, Ariano Greek 'warlike'.

Ariel, Arielo A Hebrew name. It may have meant either 'hero' or 'hearth'. In medieval Christian legends, Ariel was the name of a water spirit who was a follower of the archangel Michael. Fem: Ariela.

Aristeo Aristaeus was the Greek god of beekeeping and protector of fruit trees, from Greek *aristos* 'best, noblest'. Dim: Teo. Fem: Aristea.

Arístides Greek *aristides* 'greatest, best'. A 2nd century Greek Christian writer.

Aristófanes The name of a celebrated dramatist of classical Greece, from *aristos* 'best, noblest' + *phanein* 'to appear'.

Aristóteles Greek *aristos* 'best, noblest' + *telos* 'end, goal'. The name of a classical Greek philosopher.

Armando Germanic *hard* 'strong, brave' + *man* 'man'. Diminutive: Mando. Fem: Armanda.

Armentario, Armentaro Latin *armetarius* 'a herdsman'. Dim: Armen.

Armo A diminutive of Harmodio and Harmonio.

Arnaldo, Arnoldo Germanic *arn* 'eagle' + *wald* 'ruler'. Dims: Arne, Arni, Naldo. Catalan: Arnau. Fem: Arnalda. English: Arnold.

Arnau Catalan form of Arnaldo.

Arnulfo Germanic *arn* 'eagle' + *wulf* 'wolf'. Dim: Nulfo.

Arquibaldo see Archibaldo

Arsenio Greek *arsenios* 'energetic'. Fem: Arsenia.

Artemio, Artemón A Greek name for a devotee of Artemis, goddess of the moon and of hunting. Dim: Chemo.

Arturo This name may derive from the Celtic or Latin language. Either way, it can be traced back to *art,* an Indo-European word meaning 'a bear'. King Arthur was the hero of Celtic legends; Artorius was a Roman clan name. Dims: Art, Arti, Ito, Tur, Turi, Turín, Turo, Tuto, Tuyo. Catalan, Basque: Artur. English: Arthur.

Asterio Greek *aster* 'star'. Asteria was a Greek and Roman goddess of justice, associated with the astrological sign Virgo. Fem: Asteria.

Asunción Spanish for 'assumption'. A name given to both boys and girls in honor of La Asunción de la Virgen (the Virgin Mary's ascension into heaven). María Asunción is the patroness of the country of Paraguay. Feast August 15. Dim: Chencho.

Atahualpa 'Bird of fate' in the Quechua language of the Inca Empire. Atahualpa, the last Inca ruler of Peru, lived in the 16th century.

Atanasio Greek *athanasios* 'immortal' Dims: Tanasio, Nacho. Fem: Atanasia.

Atilano, Atiliano From a Roman name, Attilius, the origin of which is Etruscan. Its meaning is not known. San Atilano is patron of Zamora, Spain. Feast October 5. Dims: Tilán, Tilano.

Audomaro Germanic *odo* 'wealth' + *mar* 'fame'.

Augustino see Agustín

Augusto, Agosto, Agusto Latin *augustus* 'great, magnificent'. This distinguished Roman name became a title given to Roman emperors. Dims: Augie, Chucho, Tuto. Fem: Augusta. English: August.

Aulino From the Roman name Aulinus, derived from Latin *aula* 'a palace, a royal court'.

Aureliano From the Roman name Aurelianus 'a relative of Aurelius'. The name of a 3rd century Roman emperor and of a 6th century French saint. Fem: Aureliana.

Aurelio Latin *aureus* 'golden'. Diminutive: Lelio. Fem: Aurelia.

Áureo Latin *aureus* 'golden'. Feminine: Áurea.

Ausencio, Auxencio Greek *ayxis* 'to grow, to become better'. Dim: Chencho.

Austreberto Germanic *aust* 'east' + *berht* 'shining, brilliant'. Originally the name of a Visigoth sun god: Dim: Beto. Fem: Austreberta.

Avelino see Abelino

Avertano, Averano, Avertino Latin *avertere* 'to turn aside'. An early Christian name that signified turning aside from sin. Dim: Tano.

Azario, Azariel, Azarías, Ozías 'God has helped' in Hebrew. In the Bible, the name of a king of Judah.

Azul A South American name, Spanish for 'blue', a color of the Virgin Mary.

Babarito see Barbarito

Bacho A diminutive of Basilio.

Balasi Basque form of Blas.

Balbino Latin *balbus* 'stammering'. Fem: Balbina.

Baldo A diminutive of Baldomero, Baldomino and Ubaldo

Baldomero Germanic *bald* 'brave, bold' + *miru* 'protector'. Dims: Balde, Mero. Fem: Baldomera.

Baldomino, Baldomiano Hybrid names from Germanic *bald* 'brave, bold', with Latin name endings. Dim: Baldo.

Balendin Basque form of Valentín.

Baltasar Hebrew 'Bel protect the king'. Bel (Baal) was a Semitic word for 'lord, sky god'. According to medieval legends, Baltasar was one of the three Magi who carried gifts to the Christ Child (the Magi are not named in the Bible). Feast January 6. Dim: Balto. English: Balthasar.

Balto Diminutive of Baltasar, Gualterio and Walterio.

Baptista see Bautista

Barbarito, Babarito Masculine forms of Bárbara, from Latin *barbarus* 'foreigner'.

Barnabé see Bernabé

Bartolomé Hebrew 'son of Talmai'. This was the family name of Nathanael, one of the apostles. San Bartolomé (Saint Bartholomew) is the patron saint of bookbinders. Feast August 24. Dims: Barto, Bartoli, Bartolo, Toli, Tolo. Fem: Bartolomea. English: Bartholomew.

Basilio, Basileo, Basilo Greek *basileus* 'king'. Saint Basil the Great, who lived in the 4th century, was an important early Church leader. Feast January 2. Dims: Bacho, Chilo. Fem: Basilia, Basilea. English: Basil.

Bastián Originally a diminutive of Sebastián, from Greek *sebastos* 'honored'.

Baudilio, Baudillo Germanic *bald* 'bold, brave' + *hild* 'combat'. San Baudilio, who lived in the 4th century, was renowned as the builder of more than 400 churches in Spain and France. Feast May 20. Dim: Lilo.

Bautista, Baptista Greek *baptein* 'submerge, baptize'. A name bestowed in honor of San Juan Bautista (Saint John the Baptist). Feast June 24. Dims: Tito, Baucha .

Belarmino From the family name of an Italian saint, Roberto Belarmino, Jesuit and writer (1542-1641). The meaning of this name is not known. Feast September 17. Fem: Belarmina.

Belén Spanish for Bethlehem, the birthplace of Jesus. The word means 'house of bread' in Hebrew, referring to the fertile land near the town. A name bestowed in honor of the Virgin as Nuestra Señora de Belén (Our Lady of Bethlehem). Feast December 25.

Belisario Latin *belis* 'pledge'. Belisarius was a 6th century Roman general. Dims: Beliche, Chayo. Fem: Belisaria.

Beltrán, Bertrán Germanic *berht* 'shining, brilliant' + *ramm* 'raven'. The raven was sacred to the ancient god Wotan. As a Spanish first name, usually given in honor of San Luis Beltrán (1526-1581), a missionary in Central America and the Caribbean. Feast October 9. English: Bertrand.

Benicio Spanish spelling of the family name of an Italian saint, Filippo Benizzi, doctor and healer. Feast August 23.

Benigno Latin *benignus* 'kind, friendly'. Dim: Nino. Fem: Benigna.

Benildo Germanic *bern* 'a bear' + *hild* 'combat'. San Benildo was a 9th century martyr saint of Córdoba, Spain. Feast August 13.

Benito Latin *benedictus* 'blessed'. San Benito (Saint Benedict), who lived in the 6th century, founded the Benedictine Order. Feast July 11. Diminutives: Ben, Bene, Beni, Nito. Basque: Beñat. Catalan: Benet. English: Benedict, Bennett.

Benjamín Hebrew 'Son of the right hand'. In the Old Testament, Benjamin was the name of the son of Rachel and Jacob. Dims: Ben, Benny, Benji, Chemín, Micho, Min, Mincho, Mino. Fem: Benjamina. English: Benjamin.

Berenguer Germanic *bern* 'a bear' + *gar* 'spear'. The name of a knight in medieval romances about King Charlemagne. Fem: Berenguela.

Bernabé, Barnabé 'Son of encouragement' in Hebrew. In the Bible, this was the name of a companion of Saint Paul. San Bernabé (Saint Barnabas) is patron saint of peacemakers. Feast June 11. Dims: Barney, Barní. Fem: Bernabela. English: Barnaby, Barnabas.

Bernal, Bernaldo Germanic *bern* 'a bear' + *ald* 'old, venerable'. Dim: Berno.

Bernardino A hybrid name: Germanic *bern* 'a bear' + *hard* 'strong, brave', with a Latin ending. San Bernardino of Siena, Italy (1380-1444), who was famous as a preacher, is the patron saint of advertisers. Feast May 20. Dims: Bernar, Berno, Dino. Fem: Bernardina.

Bernardo Germanic *bern* 'a bear' + *hard* 'strong, brave'. The 11th century San Bernardo (Saint Bernard) of Montjoux, who was a missionary in the Alps, is patron saint of mountaineers and skiers. Feast August 20. Dims: Beño, Berna, Berno, Dino, Nardo, Nayo. Catalan: Bernard. Basque: Beiñat, Bernat. Fem: Bernarda. English: Bernard.

Bertilo, Bertilio From the Roman name Bertibilis, from Germanic *berht* 'shining, brilliant' with a Latin diminutive ending. Fem: Bertila, Bertilia.

Bertín, Bertino A blend of Germanic *berht* 'shining, brilliant' and a Latin name ending. These names are also used as diminutives of Albertín and Albertino.

Berto Germanic *berht* 'shining, brilliant'. Fem: Berta.

Berto, Beto, Veto Diminutives of the many names containing 'bert', such as Alberto, Gilberto and Roberto.

Bertoldo, Bertolo Germanic *berht* 'brilliant, shining' + *hrod* 'glory'. Dim: Berto.

Bertrán see Beltrán

Bibi A diminutive of Viviano and Bibiano.

Bibiano see Viviano

Bienvenido Spanish for 'welcomed one'. A name for a long-wished-for child. This was a popular name in the Middle Ages. Fem: Bienvenida.

Bingen, Bixintxo Basque for Vicente.

Bito A diminutive of Victor.

Bitor, Bittor Basque forms of Victor.

Biye A diminutive of Guillermo.

Bladi Basque form of Blas.

Bladimiro see Vladimiro.

Blai, Blasi Catalan forms of Blas.

Blanco From Old French *blanc* 'white, fair', signifying purity of heart. Fem: Blanca, Bianca.

Blandino Latin *blandus* 'flattering'. Dim: Dino. Fem: Blandina.

Blanio, Blano Latin *blandus* 'flattering'. English: Blain, Blane.

Blas, Blasio Latin *blaesus* 'stuttering, lisping'. San Blas (Saint Blaise), who is remembered on February 3, was a very popular saint in the Middle Ages. He is patron saint of wool workers. Catalan: Blai, Blasi. Basque: Balasi, Bladi. Fem: Blasa. English: Blaise.

Bocho A diminutive of Ambrosio and Sinforoso.

Bolívar A Basque family name, meaning 'valley of the mill'. The name is given in honor of Simón Bolívar, who led revolutions against Spain in South America. Dim: Bolo.

Bonaventura Catalan form of Buenaventura.

Bonifacio Latin *boni* 'good works' + *facio* 'to do'. The name of nine popes. Dims: Boni, Pacho. Fem: Bonifacia. English: Boniface.

Borís A shortened form of Borislav, from Slavic *bor* 'battle' + *slav* 'glory'. The name of a 10th century Russian saint.

Borja The family name of San Francisco de Borja y Aragón (1510-1572), a nobleman who left his comfortable life to become a Jesuit. Feast October 10. Fem: Borjita.

Braulio Germanic *brand* 'sword'. San Braulio, a 7th century bishop, is patron saint of Zaragoza, Spain. Feast March 26. Dim: Lalo. Fem: Braulia.

Brian An Irish royal name from Celtic *brig* 'high, noble'. Fem: Briana, Brianna, Bryana.

Bricio From the Latin name Brictius, which is derived from a Gaulish (Continental Celtic) name, the meaning of which is not known. San Bricio (Saint Brice), who lived in the 4th century, was revered throughout Europe. Fem: Bricia. English: Brice, Bryce. Bricio is also a diminutive of Fabricio.

Bruno Germanic *brun* 'brown'. San Bruno was the founder of the Carthusian Order. Feast October 6. Catalan: Bru. Basque: Burnon. Fem: Bruna. English: Bruno.

Buenaventura Spanish for 'good fortune'. A popular name in the Middle Ages, it was replaced by its diminutive, Ventura. Variant: Bonaventura.

Cachi A diminutive of Casimiro.

Cadio A diminutive of Arcadio.

Caetano see Cayetano

Caledonio see Celedonio

Calixto, Calisto Greek *kallistos* 'handsomest one'. Dim: Cali. Fem: Calixta, Calista.

Calvino From the French name Calvin, derived from Latin *calvus* 'bald'. English: Calvin.

Camerino Latin 'native of Cameria [an ancient Sabine city]'. Fem: Camerina.

Camilo In Rome, the title of a youth who assisted a priest or priestess. Dim: Camito, Milo.

Camino 'Road, path, way' in Spanish. A name for the Virgin Mary as Nuestra Señora del Camino, the protectress of travelers and pilgrims, venerated at sanctuaries in Tarragona, Spain. Feast: September 8.

Cancio, Canciano Latin *cantus* 'song'. Fem: Cancia, Canciana.

Candelario Latin *candela* 'candle'. This name is given to either a boy or a girl in honor of Candlemas, which commemorates the Holy Family's visit to the temple. Celebrated February 2. Fem: Candelaria.

Cándido Latin *candidus* 'white, shining'. Fem: Cándida.

Canuto Old Norse *knutr* 'knot', originally a nickname for a short, stout man. Saint Canute, an 11th century king of Denmark, is remembered January 19.

Cardo A diminutive of Ricardo.

Carino Greek *xarino* 'gracious'.

Carlos, Carlo Germanic *karl* 'free man'. The name of four kings of Spain. Dims: Charlie, Lito. Catalan: Carles. Basque: Xarles. Fem: Carla. English: Charles.

Carmelo Hebrew for 'vineyard'. From the name of a mountain in the Holy Land, Mount Carmel, which was dedicated to the Virgin Mary by the Carmelite monks. Dims: Carmo, Milo. Fem: Carmel, Carmela.

Carmen A variant of the name Carmel, from the Hebrew 'vineyard'. This name is given to both boys and girls in honor of Our Lady of Mt. Carmel. Its spelling has been influenced by the Spanish word *carmen*, which means 'song', and by the 19th century opera *Carmen* by Georges Bizet. As a middle name, 'del Carmen'. Feast July 16.

Casandro Masculine form of Casandra. In the *Iliad*, Cassandra was a prophetess, daughter of King Priam of Troy.

Casildo Arabic 'to sing'. The masculine form of Casilda, a saint's name. A shrine and a pool near Burgos, Spain, are dedicated to Santa Casilda, and couples who wish to have children toss stones into the pool.

Casiano From Cassius, the name of a Roman clan, derived from Latin *cassi* 'metal helmet'. San Casiano was a 3rd century martyr. Feast April 16. Fem: Casiana.

Casimiro Spanish version of the Polish name Kazimierz, derived from Slavic *kasic* 'to destroy' + *meri* 'great'. King Casimir was king Poland in the 15th century, is patron saint of Poland, of Lithuania and of princes. Feast March 4. Dims: Cachi, Miro. Fem: Casimira.

Casio From Cassius, name of a Roman clan, derived from Latin *cassi* 'metal helmet'. Fem: Casia.

Casiodoro Greek *kasios* 'brother' + *doron* 'gift' = 'brother's gift'.

Casto Latin *castus* 'clean, pure'. A name used by early Christians. Also a diminutive of Cástoro. Fem: Casta.

Cástoro, Castor Greek *castor* 'beaver'. A name from Greek myth. Castor and Pollux are the twins of the constellation Gemini. San Cástoro, who was an early martyr, is patron saint of sculptors. Feast November 8. Dim: Casto. Fem: Cástora.

Cástulo From a Latin name, a diminutive of *castus* 'clean, pure'. Dim: Tulo.

Catalino, Catarino Masculine forms of Catalina and Catarina, from Greek *katharos* 'pure'. Dim: Lino.

Cayetano, Caetano, Gayetano, Gaetano Latin *Caietanus* 'a native of Caetia [a city in central Italy]'. Dims: Cayo, Tano. Fem: Cayetana, Gayetana.

Cayo Latin Gaius, one of the most popular men's first names in ancient Rome. Its origin is not known. Cayo is also used as a diminutive of Cayetano and Ricario.

Cebrián see Cipriano

Cecilio From Caecilius, a Roman clan name, derived from Latin *caecus* 'blind'. Although there is an obscure 3rd century San Cecilio, the popularity of this name is due to widespread veneration of Santa Cecilia (Saint Cecilia). Dims: Cecil, Celio, Cilio. Fem: Cecilia. English: Cecil.

Cedro A diminutive of Isidro.

Ceferino, Zeferino Latin *zepherinus* 'west wind'. Name of the 3rd pope. Dims: Cefero, Chefino, Fino. Fem: Ceferina.

Celedonio, Caledonio Greek *chelidonon* 'swallow [the bird]'. Feast March 3. Fem: Celedonia, Caledonia.

Celerino Latin *celer* 'fast, swift'. Fem: Celerina.

Celestino Latin *caelestis* 'heavenly'. The name of five popes. Dim: Tino. Fem: Celeste, Celestina.

Celino, Celín From the Roman name Caelinus 'a relative of Caelius', derived from Latin *caelum* 'sky, heaven'. Fem: Celina.

Celio From a Roman clan name, Caelius, derived from Latin *caelum* 'heaven, sky'. Dims: Celín, Chelo. Fem: Celia.

Celso Latin *celsus* 'lofty, high'. Fem: Celsa.

Cenobio see Zenobio

César, Cesar, Cesaro From the Roman family name Caesar, possibly from Latin *caesaries* 'having abundant hair'. Julius Caesar was a celebrated Roman general and leader. Later, the word 'Caesar' was used as a title for all Roman emperors. Dims: Chayo, Sarito. Basque: Kesar. Fem: Cesarina.

Cesáreo, Cesario, Cesarión Latin Cesareus 'a relative of Caesar'. Fem: Cesaria, Cesárea.

Chaco A diminutive of Ezequiel.

Chago A diminutive of Jacobo and Santiago.

Chan, Chano Diminutives of Juan.

Chano A diminutive of names ending in '-ano', such as Marciano and Sebastiano.

Chanti, Chango Diminutives of Santiago.

Chava A diminutive of Salvador.

Chavo A diminutive of Gustavo and Salvador.

Chayo A diminutive of Belisario and César.

Che, Chelín Diminutives of José.

Chebo A diminutive of Eusebio and Sebastián.

Cheche A diminutive of Moisés.

Checo A diminutive of Ezequías, Ezequiel and Hesiquio.

Chefino A diminutive of Ceferino.

Chelino A diminutive of Marcelino.

Chelmo A diminutive of Anselmo.

Chelo A diminutive of Celio, Marcelo.

Chemín A diminutive of Benjamín.

Chemo A diminutive of Antemio and Artemio.

Chenche, Chente Dims. of Vicente.

Chencho A diminutive of Crescencio, Lorenzo, Fulgencio and Inocencio.

Chendo A diminutive of Rosendo.

Cheno A diminutive of Eugenio.

Chente A diminutive of Inocente.

Cheo A diminutive of Amadeo and Eliseo.

Chepe, Chepo Diminutives of José.

Chequelo A diminutive of Ezequiel.

Cheto A diminutive of Aniceto.

Chico, Chicho Diminutives of Narciso.

Chilano A diminutive of Maximiliano.

Chilo A diminutive of Basilio.

Chindo A diminutive of Gumersindo.

Chinto A diminutive of Jacinto.

Chiro A diminutive of Isidro.

Chivi A diminutive of Silvio.

Chomín A diminutive of Domingo.

Chomo A diminutive of Jerónimo.

Chu, Chuey, Chus, Chuy Diminutives of Jesús.

Chucho A diminutive of Augusto.

Cicerón Latin *cicero* 'garbanzo bean'. Marcus Tullius Cicero was a great Roman orator.

Cipriano, Cebrián Latin *Cyprianus* 'a native of the island of Cyprus'. From the Sumerian word for 'copper', a mineral mined on the island from ancient times. San Cipriano (Saint Cyprian), a 3rd century bishop of Carthage, was an important early Church writer. Feast September 16. Dims: Chano, Cip, Piano. Fem: Cipriana.

Cireneo, Cirino, Cirión Latin 'a native of Cyrene [a Greek city in North Africa]'. From the name a nymph in Greek myth. Dim: Ciro. Fem: Cirenea, Cirenia.

Ciriáco see Quirze

Cirilo Greek *kyrios* 'master'. In the 9th century, San Cirilo (Saint Cyril) evangelized eastern Europe and developed the Cyrillic alphabet to translate the Bible. Feast February 14. Dims: Cirio, Ciro, Lilo. Fem: Cirila. English: Cyril.

Cirino, Cirión see Cireneo

Ciro Greek *kyrios* 'master'. Also a diminutive of Cireneo and Cirilo. Fem: Cira.

Cisco A diminutive of Francisco.

Claro, Clario Latin *clarus* 'bright, clear'. Fem: Clara.

Claudino Latin 'a relative of Claudius'. Fem: Claudina.

Claudio From Claudius, a Roman name derived from Latin *claudus* 'lame'. It was the name of two Roman emperors. Fem: Claudia. English: Claude.

Cleandro Greek *kleos* 'glory' + *andros* 'of man'. The name of a lieutenant of Alexander the Great.

Clemencio Latin *clementia* 'mercy'. Fem: Clemencia.

Clemente, Clementino Latin *clemens, clementis* 'merciful'. The name of a disciple of Saint Paul and of fourteen popes. Dims: Cleme, Mente, Tente, Tino. Fem: Clementina. English: Clement.

Cleofás Greek *kleo* 'to celebrate' + *phasis* 'the rising of a star'. Fem: Cleofé.

Cleto A diminutive of Anacleto.

Clodomiro Germanic *hrod* 'glory' + *miru* 'protector'. Dims: Clodo, Miro. Fem: Clodomira.

Clodoveo Germanic *hrod* 'glory' + *wig* 'warrior', the same source as the name Luis. Dim: Clodo. Fem: Clodovea.

Coco, Cocoy Diminutives of Jorge.

Cola, Colas Diminutives of Nicolás.

Colón, Colomo Latin *columba* 'a dove'. The Irish San Colomo (Saint Columba), an early Irish missionary to Scotland, is patron saint of poets. Feast June 9. Fem: Paloma, Coloma.

Conrado Germanic *kuon* 'bold' + *rad* 'advice, counsel'. English: Conrad.

Constancio, Constante Latin *constantia* 'perseverance, steadfastness'. Diminutives: Conso, Stancio, Stanzo. Fem: Constancia, Constanza, Constanta.

Constantino Latin Constantinus, a Roman family name, from Latin *constantia* 'perseverance, steadfastness'. Constantine was the first Roman emperor to accept Christianity. Dim: Tino. Fem: Constantina. English: Constantine.

Coque A diminutive of Jorge.

Cornelio From the Roman family name Cornelius, derived from Latin *cornelium* 'little horn'. In the New Testament, this was the name of a Roman soldier who was converted by Saint Peter. Dim: Nelo. Fem: Cornelia. English: Cornelius.

Cosme Greek *kosmas* 'order, beauty'. San Cosme, along with his twin brother, San Damián, is patron saint of doctors, pharmacists, barbers and hairdressers. Feast September 26. Fem: Cósima.

Crescencio Latin *crescens* 'growing'. A name created by early Christians to describe their growing faith. Dims: Chencho, Crescito. Fem: Crescencia.

Cris A diminutive of 'Cris-' names.

Crisanto Greek *krisos* 'gold' + *anthos* 'flower' = 'golden flower, chrysanthemum'. Dims: Cris, Santito, Santo. Fem: Crisantemo.

Crisóforo Greek *krisos* 'gold' + *phoros* 'to carry'. Dim: Cris.

Crisógono Greek *krisos* 'gold' + *gono* 'creator, maker'. Dim: Cris.

Crisólogo Greek *krisos* 'golden' + *logos* 'words'.

Crispín, Crispino, Crispiano From the Roman name Crispinus, derived from Latin *crispus* 'curly-haired'. San Crispín, a 3rd century martyr, was a very popular saint in the Middle Ages. Feast November 19. Dims: Cris, Pino. Fem: Crispina. English: Crispin.

Cristián, Cristiano Latin *Christianus* 'a follower of Christ'. Fem: Cristina, Cristiana. English: Christian.

Cristóbal, Cristóforo, Cristofer Greek *Khristos* 'Christ' + *pherein* 'carry' = 'carrier of Christ'. A name created by the early Christians to signify that they carried Christ in their hearts. According to legend, San Cristóbal (Saint Christopher), a pagan giant, carried Christ across a river and was converted to Christianity. Until 1969, when he was removed from the official company of saints, Christopher was the popular patron saint of travelers, invoked for protection against accidents. Feast July 25. Dims: Cris, Cristo, Chris, Tobal, Tobalito. Catalan: Cristòfol. Fem: Cristolbina. English: Christopher.

Cruz Latin *crux, crucis* 'cross'. A name created by early Christians, signifying the death of Christ on the cross. As a middle name, 'de la Cruz' or 'de la Santa Cruz'. Feast of La Exaltación de la Santa Cruz September 14.

Cuarto Latin *quartus* 'fourth'. A name given to a fourth son.

Cuauhtémoc 'Descending eagle' in the Náhuatl language of Mexico. A name given in honor of the last Aztec emperor.

Cuco A diminutive of Refugio.

Cugat The Catalan form of the name of Cucuphas of Africa, a 3rd century saint martyred in Barcelona. Feast July 25.

Cuitláhuac A name given in honor of an Aztec ruler who was the nephew of Moctezuma.

Curcio Latin *curtus* 'short'.

Curro A diminutive of Francisco.

Custodio A name from early Christian times, 'guardian angel' in Latin. La Fiesta de los Ángeles Custodios is celebrated on October 2. Dim: Toyo. Fem: Custodia.

Cutberto Old English *cuth* 'famous' + *beorht* 'bright'. Saint Cuthbert was a 7th century English saint revered throughout Europe for his miracles. Feast March 20.

Dabi Basque form of David.

Dacio Latin 'a native of Dacia [a region in the lower Danube in present-day Rumania]'. From *daos* 'wolf' in a dialect of ancient Greek. Fem: Dacia.

Dagoberto Germanic *dag* 'day' + *berht* 'shining, brilliant'. Dim: Berto.

Dalmacio Latin 'a native Dalmatia', a region on the Adriatic Sea. The name is from Indo-European *dhal* 'young animal'. Catalan: Dalmai, Dalmau. Fem: Dalmacia.

Dalmiro see Adelmaro

Dámaso Greek *damasos* 'animal tamer'. San Dámaso was a fourth century pope. Feast December 11.

Damián, Damiano From the name of the goddess Damia, otherwise known as Cybele, who was widely worshipped in the Mediterranean area in ancient times. Along with his twin brother San Cosme, San Damiano is the patron saint of doctors, pharmacists, hairdressers and barbers. Feast September 26. Dims: Dami, Damito. Fem: Damiana. English: Damian.

Daniel, Danil, Danilo A hero of the Old Testament. The name means 'God is my judge' in Hebrew. Dims: Dani, Dany, Danny, Nel, Nelo, Nilo. Fem: Daniela, Danela, Danila. Basque: Danel. English: Daniel.

Dante A diminutive of Durante, from Latin *durans* 'continuing, enduring'. The name was popularized by the Italian poet Dante Alighieri (1265-1321).

Darío Persian *darayaraus* 'active'. Name of a Persian emperor. Dims: Dari, Dayo. Fem: Daria. English: Darius.

David Hebrew 'beloved'. In the Bible, the name of a great king of Israel. Dims: Davi, Davito. Basque: Dabi. Fem: Davidia, Davina, Davita. English: David.

Delfín, Delfino Greek Delphinia, an epithet of the goddess Artemis at her shrine on the island of Delphi. The word is derived from Greek *delphis* 'dolphin'. Dims: Delfi, Delfito, Fino. Fem: Delfina.

Delmar, Delmaro, Delmiro, Demario see Adelmaro

Demetrio Greek *Demetrios* 'devotee of Demeter [the Greek mother goddess]'. This name was borne by 53 saints. Dims: Déme, Mecho, Meti. Fem: Demetria, Demetra. English: Demetrius.

Deodato Latin *deodatus* 'gift of God'.

Deseado Spanish for 'desired'.

Desiderio, Desiderato Latin *desiderium* 'longing', a name created by early Christians to describe their longing for Christ. Dim: Desi. Fem: Desideria.

Deunoro Basque form of Santo, Santos.

Dídimo Greek *didymos* 'twin', another name for the apostle San Tomás (Saint Thomas). Dim: Didi.

Diego In the Middle Ages, the name Sant Yago (the Spanish form of Saint James) was misunderstood by some as 'San Tiago', and this morphed into 'San Diego'. Thus, the names Santiago, Diego and Jaime are all from the same source. San Diego de Alcalá, the patron saint of cooks, is remembered on November 13. Catalan: Dídac. Basque: Didaka. Dim: Dieguín. Fem: Diega. English: James. See also Santiago and Jaime.

Dino A diminutive of Blandino and Dionisio.

Diodoro Latin form of the Greek name Teodoro: *theos* 'God' + *doron* 'gift' = 'gift of God'. Dims: Dito, Doro.

Dión A diminutive of Dionisio.

Dionisio Greek Dionysios, the god of wine and festivals. The meaning of the name is not known. San Dionisio (Saint Denis in French), an early evangelist, is the patron saint of Paris. Feast October 9. Dims: Dino, Dión, Nicho, Nisio. Catalan: Dionís. Basque: Dunixi. Fem: Dionisia, Dionisa, Denisa. English: Dennis.

Diosdado Spanish for 'gift of God'.

Dolfo A diminutive of Adolfo.

Domenico see Domingo

Domiciano From a Roman clan name, Domitius, derived from the Latin *domus* 'house, home'. Dims: Domi, Domico, Chano.

Dominador 'Dominating, powerful' in Spanish.

Domingo, Domenico From Dominicus, a Late Latin name which is derived from Latin *dominus* 'lord'. The Spanish Santo Domingo (Saint Dominic, 1170-1221), was the founder of the Dominican Order. He is patron saint of astronomers. Feast August 8. Dims: Chomín, Mingo. Basque: Txomin. Fem: Dominga. English: Dominic, Dominick.

Domitilo From Latin *domitor* 'one who tames'. Dim: Tilo. Fem: Domitila.

Donaldo Spanish form of the Scottish name Donald, from Celtic *dumno-valos* 'world king'.

Donato Latin *donatus* 'given [by God]'. Dim: Nato. Fem: Donatela, Donatila.

Donoso Latin *donus* 'gift'. Dims: Dono, Nosito, Noso. Fem: Donosa.

Doro A diminutive of Doroteo, Heliodoro, Isidoro and Teodoro.

Doroteo Greek *doron* 'gift' + *theos* 'God' = 'gift of God'. Dims: Doro, Teo. Fem: Dorotea.

Draconte, Dragón Greek *drakon* 'serpent, dragon'.

Duarte Originally, this was a diminutive of Eduardo.

Dunixi Basque form of Dionisio.

Durán, Durante, Durando From Latin *durans* 'enduring'. Dims: Dante, Rante, Rantito

Eberardo see Everardo

Edelberto see Adelberto

Edelmaro, Edelmiro see Adelmaro

Edgar, Edgardo Anglo-Saxon *ead* 'rich, happy' + *gar* 'spear'. A British royal name.

Edilberto see Adalberto

Edilio Germanic *adal* 'noble'.

Edmundo Anglo-Saxon *ead* 'happy, rich' + *mund* 'protection'. The name of a 9th century British king and martyr saint who was venerated throughout Europe. Dims: Eddie, Mundo. English: Edmund.

Eduardo, Duarte Anglo-Saxon *ead* 'rich, happy' + *weard* 'guardian'. King Edward 1 of England took a Spanish wife, Eleanor of Castille. Dims: Duardo, Duarte, Eddy, Lalo. Catalan: Eduard. Basque: Edorta. Fem: Eduarda. English: Edward.

Eduino Anglo-Saxon *ead* 'rich, happy' + *win* 'friend'. The name of a 7th century British king and martyr saint.

Efraín, Efrén, Efreín, Afraín Hebrew 'a native of Ephron [a village in Palestine]'. Ephron means 'fruitful place'. Dims: Efra, Juncho, Juincho. English: Ephraim.

Egidio Greek *aigidios* 'goat, kid'. San Egidio was an 8th century miracle worker venerated throughout Europe. He is the patron saint of hermits, beggars and blacksmiths. Feast September 1. Dim: Gil. Fem: Egidia. English: Giles.

Eladio From the Greek name Heladio 'a native of Helas, a Greek person'. San Eladio, founder of a 7th century monastery, is patron saint of the physically disabled. Feast February 18. Fem: Eladia.

Eleazar, Eleázaro, Elizario, Eliazar, Eliecer, Elzear, Elzeario Hebrew 'God, my help'. In the Bible, a high priest in the time of Moses.

Eleodoro, Eleadoro, Heliodoro Greek *helios* 'sun' + *doron* 'gift'.

Eleuterio Latin *Eleutherias* 'liberating', epithet of Jupiter, the Roman god of sky and thunder. Dims: Teo, Teyo.

Eli Hebrew 'God is exalted'. In the Old Testament, Eli was a judge and high priest of Israel.

Eliades Greek *heliades* 'son of the sun'.

Elián, Eliano Greek *helios* 'sun'. Dim: Elio. Fem: Eliana, Heliana.

Elías Hebrew 'God is Lord'. The Spanish equivalent of Elijah, one of the great prophets of the Old Testament. Fem: Elia. English: Elias, Elijah.

Eliázar, Eliecer see Eleázar

Eligio, Eligeo Latin *eligius* 'chosen, elected'. San Eligio (Saint Eligius), who lived in the 6th century, is the patron saint of silversmiths and goldsmiths. Feast December 1. Dim: Kiko.

Elija Variant of Elías.

Elipidio, Elpidio Latin *elipidius* 'hope'.

Elisardo, Lisardo, Lizardo Used as masculine forms of Elizabeth, these names were probably originally forms of Eleazar or Eliseo, with the addition of the Germanic name-element *hard* 'strong, brave'.

Eliseo 'God is salvation' in Hebrew. The name of an Old Testament prophet. Dim: Cheo, Licha. English: Elisha.

Elizario, Elzear, Elzeario see Eleázar

Elmo see Telmo

Eloi, Eloy Catalan forms of Eligio.

Elpidio see Elipidio

Emanuel, Emmanuel 'God is with us' in Hebrew. In the Bible, the name for the promised Messiah. The modern Spanish form of this name is Manuel. Dim: Manny. Basque: Imanel. Fem: Emanuela. English: Emanuel.

Emerenciano Latin *emerere* 'earned'.

Emérito Latin *emeritus* 'retired person, veteran'. Many veterans of the Roman army were granted land in the territory that is now Spain. Fem: Emérita.

Emilián, Emiliano From the Roman clan name, Aemilianus 'a relative of Aemilius', derived from Latin *aemulus* 'rival'. Dim: Emil. Fem: Emiliana.

Emilio, Emilo From the Roman clan name, Aemilius, derived from Latin *aemulus* 'rival'. Dims: Melo, Milo. Fem: Emilia. English: Emile.

Eneas Greek *aineias* 'worthy of praise'. Aeneas, the legendary founder of Rome, was the hero of the *Aeneid* by the Roman poet Virgil.

Enrique Germanic *haim* 'home' + *ric* 'king'. Dims: Kiki, Kiko, Quico, Quique. Catalan: Enric. Basque: Endika. Fem: Enrica, Enriqueta. English: Henry.

Epifanio Latin *epiphanius* 'epiphany'. A name used by early Christians, commemorating the Feast of the Epiphany, January 6. Dim: Pifano. Fem: Epifana, Epifanía.

Erardo, Herardo Germanic *heri* 'army' + *hard* 'strong, brave'.

Erasmo Greek *erasmios* 'beloved'. San Erasmo (Saint Erasmus), was a 3rd century martyr, the patron saint of sailors. Another Erasmus was a 15th century Dutch humanist whose writings inspired a spiritual movement in Spain.

Erberto, Eriberto see Herberto.

Erico, Érico Germanic *ehren* 'honor' + *ric* 'king'. Fem: Erica. English: Eric.

Erminio see Herminio

Ernestino A blended name from Germanic *ernst* 'strength, vigor', with a Latin ending. Fem: Ernestina.

Ernesto Germanic *ernst* 'strength, vigor'. Diminutives: Ernio, Necho, Nesti, Nesto. Fem: Ernesta, Ernestina. English: Ernest.

Erramun Basque form of Ramón.

Errando Basque form of Fernando.

Erricarta Basque form of Ricardo.

Estanislao Slavic *stan* 'government' + *slav* 'a Slav'. San Estanislao (Saint Stanislas) was an 11th century Polish martyr who was revered throughout Europe. Feast May 7. Dims: Lalo, Tanas, Tani. Fem: Estanislada.

Esteban, Estevan, Estefan, Estefano Greek *stephanos* 'victorious'. San Esteban (Saint Stephen) was the first Christian martyr. Feast December 26. Dim: Tebe. Catalan: Esteve. Basque: Eztebe. Fem: Estefania. English: Stephen, Steven.

Etelvino Germanic *adal* 'noble' + *win* 'friend'. Fem: Etelvina.

Eudosio, Eudoxio Greek *eu* 'good' + *doxa* 'opinion, reputation'. Fem: Eudosia, Eudoxia.

Eufemio Greek *eu phenai* 'good speaker'. Fem: Eufemia.

Eugenio Greek *eugenes* 'well-born, noble'. San Eugenio of Tolédo, Spain, was a 7th century writer and composer of music. Feast November 13. Dims: Cheno, Geni, Genio, Geño, Queño. Fem: Eugenia. English: Eugene.

Eulalio Greek *eu* 'good, well' + *lalios* 'to speak'. Dim: Lalo. Fem: Eulalia.

Eulogio Greek *eu* 'good, well' + *logos* 'thought'. San Eulogio of Córdoba, Spain, is remembered January 9. Dims: Locho, Lolo, Loyo. Fem: Eulogia.

Eusebio Greek *eusebeia* 'piety'. Dim: Chebo. Fem: Eusebia.

Eustaquio, Eustacio, Eustasio Greek *eu* 'good' + *stakhys* 'sword'. San Eustaquio, the patron saint of Madrid, was a 2nd century Roman soldier who converted to Christianity after he saw a vision of the cross between the horns of a stag he was hunting. Feast September 20. Dim: Tajo. Fem: Eustaquia, Eustasia, Eustacia.

Evangelino Greek *euangelion* 'good news'. Fem: Evangelina.

Evangelista Greek *euangelos* 'bringing good news'. A name bestowed in honor of Saint John the Evangelist.

Evaristo Greek *eu* 'good' + *aristos* 'best, noblest'. The name of the fourth pope. Fem: Evarista.

Evelio A masculine form of Eva or Evelia.

Everardo Germanic *eber* 'wild boar' + *hard* 'strong, brave'. Dim: Lalo. English: Everard.

Ezequiel, Ezequías, Exequías, Hesiquio Hebrew 'God gives strength'. The name of a prophet and of a book of the Old Testament. Dims: Checo, Chequelo, Quelo, Sequel.

Eztebe Basque form of Esteban.

Fabián, Fabiano From a Roman name, Fabianus 'a relative of Fabius', derived from Latin *faba* 'bean'. Dim: Nano. Fem: Fabia. English: Fabian.

Fabio From a Roman clan name, Fabius, derived from Latin *faba* 'bean'. Catalan: Fabi, Favi. Basque: Pavi. Fem: Fabia.

Fabriciano From the Roman name Fabricianus 'a relative of Fabricius', derived from Latin *fabrica* 'arts and crafts'. Fem: Fabriciana.

Fabricio From the Roman clan name Fabricius, derived from Latin *fabrica* 'arts and crafts'. Dim: Bricio. Fem: Fabricia.

Facundo Latin *facundia* 'eloquence'. Fem: Facunda.

Fafa, Falo, Fallo Diminutives of Rafael.

Falco, Falcón This name may be from Germanic *fulc* 'people' or from a Late Latin word meaning 'falcon'.

Faron, Faraón, Faro Egyptian 'father' (Pharaoh in English). Fem: Fara.

Farruco Galician form of Francisco.

Faustino Latin *faustus* 'lucky, favorable'. Dim: Tino. Fem: Faustina.

Fausto Latin *faustus* 'lucky, favorable'. Fem: Fausta.

Federico Germanic *fridu* 'peace' + *ric* 'king'. Dims: Fede, Fredi, Freddy, Kiko. Catalan: Frederic. Basque: Frederik, Perderika. Fem: Federica, Fedrica. English: Frederick.

Feliciano Latin *felix* 'fortunate, lucky'. Dim: Chano. Fem: Feliciana.

Felipe Greek *philein* 'to love' + *hippos* 'horses'. A name borne by many Spanish kings. San Felipe the Apostle is patron saint of Uruguay, hat makers and pastry chefs. Feast May 3. Dims: Felo, Lipe, Lipo, Pepe. Fem: Felipa. English: Philip, Phillip.

Félix Latin *felix* 'fortunate, lucky'. The name of 4 popes. Catalan: Feliu. Basque: Peli. Fem: Felisa. English: Felix.

Felo A diminutive of Felipe and Rafael.

Ferdinando see Fernando

Fermín Latin *firmus* 'firm, strong'. Dims: Min, Mincho. Fem: Fermina.

Fernando, Fernán, Ferdinando Germanic *fridu* 'peace' + *nand* 'ready, prepared'. A Spanish royal name. San Fernando (King Ferdinand III of Castille, 1198-1252) is patron saint of kings, governors and prisoners. Feast May 30. Dims: Ferdi, Nando, Nano. Catalan: Ferran. Basque: Perrando, Errando. Fem: Fernanda, Ferdinanda. English: Ferdinand.

Fero A diminutive of '-fredo' names.

Ferran Catalan form of Fernando.

Fidel, Fidelio, Fidelino Latin *fidelis* 'faithful, honest'. Fem: Fidelia, Fidela, Fidelina.

Fidencio Latin *fidentia* 'confidence'.

Filemón, Filomeno Greek *philos* 'friend' + *menos* 'strength'. San Filemón is the patron saint of dancers. Feast March 21. Dim: Meno. Fem: Filomena.

Filiberto Germanic *filu* 'much' + *berht* 'shining, brilliant'. Dim: Berto. English: Philbert.

Filo A diminutive of Teófilo.

Filomeno see Filemón

Firo A diminutive of Porfirio.

Fito A diminutive of names with an 'f' near the end, such as Adolfo and Serafín.

Flaviano From the Roman name Flavianus 'relative of Flavius', derived from Latin *flavus* 'yellow'. Fem: Flaviana.

Flavio From a Roman clan name, Flavius, derived from Latin *flavus* 'yellow'. Fem: Flavia.

Florencio, Florente Latin *florens* 'flowering'. Dim: Lencho. Fem: Florencia.

Florentín, Florentino From the Roman name Florentinus 'a native of Florence'. Dim: Tino. Fem: Florentina.

Florián, Floriano Latin *flos, floris* 'a flower'. San Florián, the patron saint of Austria, of Poland, and of firemen, was a 4th century Roman saint. He is invoked for protection against floods. Feast May 4. Fem: Floriana.

Florido Latin *floridus* 'flowery'. Fem: Florida.

Florino, Florinio Latin *flos, floris* 'a flower'. Fem: Florina, Florinia.

Fonso A diminutive of Alfonso.

Foro A diminutive of Sinforoso.

Fortiano, Fortán From the Roman clan name Fortianus, derived from Latin *fortis* 'strong, powerful'.

Fortino Latin *fortis* 'strong, powerful'.

Fortunato Latin *fortunatus* 'lucky, fortunate'. Fem: Fortunata.

Fortuno, Fortunio, Fortuño Latin *fortuna* 'luck, chance'. Dims: Tuni, Tuño. Fem: Fortuna.

Francisco, Francesco Latin *Franciscus* 'a Frenchman'. San Francisco de Asis (Saint Francis of Assisi) is the patron saint of Italy; of San Francisco, California; of Santa Fe, New Mexico; and also of zoos, animals and ecologists. As a child, he was given the nickname Franciscus because he could speak French. Feast October 4. Dims: Cisco, Curro, Franco, Frascuelo, Frasquito, Paco, Pancho, Paquito, Quico, Quito. Fem: Francisca, Francesca. Catalan: Francesc. Basque: Prantxes. English: Francis.

Franco Germanic *franc* 'a Frank'. The Franks, a Germanic-speaking tribe, invaded the western Roman Empire in the 5th century. Fem: Franca. English: Frank.

Frederico see Federico

Fredi, Fredo, Fredy Diminutives of Alfredo and Federico.

Froilán Germanic *franji* 'nobleman'. San Froilán was a 9th century archbishop of León, Spain. Feast October 5.

Fucho, Fujo Diminutives of Refugio.

Fulgencio Latin *fulgentius* 'flashing light, lightning'. San Fulgencio, a 7th century Spanish bishop, is patron saint of Cartagena and Murcia, Spain. Feast January 16. Dim: Chencho. Fem: Fulgencia.

Fulvio Latin Fulvius, name of a Roman clan, derived from *fulvus* 'yellow-brown'. Fem: Fulvia.

Gabe, Gabi Diminutives of Gabriel.

Gabino, Gabinio Latin Gabinius 'native of Gabio [an ancient city near Rome]'. Fem: Gabina.

Gabriel, Gabrielo Hebrew 'a man of God'. In the Bible, it was the archangel Gabriel who told Mary that she would bear the Christ Child. As San Gabriel, he is the patron saint of diplomats, postal workers and stamp collectors. Feast September 29. Dims: Bel, Gabe, Gabi, Gabio, Gabrio, Gaby, Lelo. Basque: Gabirel. Fem: Gabriela. English: Gabriel.

Gaetano see Cayetano

Gaizka Basque form of Salvador.

Galeno Greek *galenos* 'serene, calm', the name of a physician and philosopher of 2nd century BC Athens. Fem: Galena, Galenia. English: Galen.

Gamaliel 'God has rewarded me' in Hebrew. In the Bible, the name of a teacher of Paul of Tarsus. Feast August 3. Dim: Gamal.

García This Basque name was once a first name, but is now more commonly a last name. Its meaning is not known. 'Fox' and 'bear' are possibilities.

Garcilaso This name probably has the same Basque source as García. Garcilaso de la Vega (1501-1536) was a Spanish poet. A different Garcilaso de la Vega (1539-1616) was a historian.

Garibaldi, Garibaldo Germanic *gar* 'spear' + *bald* 'daring, bold'. A name given in honor of the Italian patriot, Giuseppe Garibaldi (1807-1882), who fought in South American wars of independence.

Gaspar A name of uncertain origin, perhaps Persian. In medieval popular tradition, Gaspar was one of the three Magi who carried gifts to the Christ Child. Feast January 6. Fem: Gaspara. English: Caspar, Jasper.

Gastón Germanic *gast* 'host', by way of the French name, Gaston.

Gayetano see Cayetano

Gela, Geyo Diminutives of Rogelio.

Gelo, Gelito Diminutives of Ángel.

Genaro, Jenaro Latin Ianuarius, name of the Roman god of beginnings and of the new year. Dim: Jano. Fem: Genara, Jenara.

Genciano Latin *gentiana* 'gentian'. The name for a mountain plant that has blue or purple flowers. Fem: Genciana.

Generoso Latin *generosus* 'of noble birth'. Dim: Gene. Fem: Generosa.

Genesión see Ginés

Geni, Genio, Geñi, Geño Diminutives of Eugenio.

Geraldo Germanic *gar* 'spear' + *wald* 'ruler, governor'. Dim: Lalo. Fem: Geraldina. English: Gerald.

Gerardo Germanic *gar* 'a spear' + *hard* 'brave, strong'. Diminutive: Gero. Catalan: Gerard, Grau. Basque: Kerarta. Fem: Gerarda, Gerardina. English: Gerard.

Gergori see Gregorio.

Germán, Germano, Jermán, Jermano Late Latin *germanus* 'brother', from the name of a 4th century French saint (Saint Germain in French). Dim: Manche. Fem: Germana. English: Herman.

Gerónimo The Spanish name of a famous Apache Indian chief. A variant of Jerónimo.

Gervasio, Gervaso Spanish form of the medieval French name, Gervais, from Germanic *gar* 'spear'. Fem: Gervasia. English: Jarvis, Gervais, Gervase.

Gesualdo Germanic *gisil* 'pledge' + *wald* 'ruler, governor'.

Gigo A diminutive of Rodrigo.

Gil Originally a diminutive of Egidio. According to legend, this Greek Saint fled to France and became a hermit because his miracles attracted too much attention in his native land. Catalan: Geli, Gelis. English: Giles.

Gilamu Basque form of Guillermo.

Gilberto, Gisberto Germanic *gisil* 'a pledge' + *berht* 'shining, brilliant'. Dims: Gil, Berto, Beto. Fem: Gilberta. English: Gilbert.

Gildo A diminutive of Hermenegildo.

Gillermo see Guillermo

Gilo A diminutive of Virgilio.

Ginés, Genesio Latin *genus* 'origin'. Genesius, who lived in the 3rd century, is the patron saint of actors and comedians. Feast August 25. Fem: Ginesa.

Ginio A diminutive of Higinio.

Giraldo see Geraldo

Gisberto see Gilberto

Godofredo, Godfredo Germanic *gott* 'god' + *fridu* 'peace'. Dim: Fero. Catalan: Jofre, Guifré. English: Godfrey.

Gonzalo, González Germanic *gundi* 'war' + *al* 'all'. Dims: Chalo, Gonsito, Gonzo, Lalo. Catalan: Goncal. Basque: Gontzal.

Gorka Basque form of Jorge.

Gotzon Basque form of Angelo.

Gracián, Graciano From a Roman clan name, Gratianus, derived from Latin *gratius* 'charming, pleasant'. Dim: Chano. Fem: Graciana.

Graciliano From a Roman clan name, Gracilianus, derived from Latin *gratia* 'grace'. Fem: Graciliana.

Grau Catalan form of Gerardo.

Gregorio, Gergori Greek *gregorios* 'vigilant, watchful'. The name of sixteen popes, including Gregory the Great (ca 540-604), patron saint of masons, teachers, singers and musicians. Feast January 2. Dims: Gollo, Goyo, Orio. Fem: Gregorina. English: Gregory.

Guadalupe Arabic *wadi* 'river' + Latin *lupus* 'wolf'. A name given to both boys and girls. There are two sanctuaries of the Virgin Mary by this name. The earlier Guadalupe is in Cáceres, Spain. It was founded by San Leandro and contains an image of the Virgin Mary. The second is at a site in Mexico where the Virgin appeared to a native man, Juan Diego, in 1531. Our Lady of Guadalupe is patroness of Mexico and the Americas. Feast December 12.

Gualberto Germanic *wald* 'ruler, governor' + *berht* 'shining, brilliant'. Dims: Berto, Beto.

Gualterio, Gutierre, Walterio Germanic *wald* 'ruler, governor' + *heri* 'army'. Dim: Balto. English: Walter.

Guido Germanic *witu* 'wide'. English: Guy.

Guifré Catalan form of Godofredo.

Guillem A Catalan form of Guillermo and a popular name in the Catalunya region of Spain.

Guillermo, Guillermino Germanic *will* 'will' + *helm* 'protector'. Dims: Guille, Guillo, Llemo, Memo, Mino. Catalan: Guillem. Basque: Gilamu. Fem: Guillerma, Guillermina. English: William.

Gumersindo Germanic *guma* 'man' + *sind* 'path'. A traditional Galician name. San Gumersindo, a 9th century martyr saint of Córdoba, Spain, is remembered January 13. Dims: Gume, Chindo. Fem: Gumersinda.

Gurutz Basque form of Cruz.

Gustavo Old Norse *gautr* 'a Goth' + *stafr* 'staff'. Dims: Chavo, Tavín, Tavo. Fem: Gustava. English: Gustaf, Gustav.

Gutierre see Gualterio

Guzmán Germanic *gothsmann* 'a nobleman'.

Harmodio, Harmonio Greek *harmodios* 'harmonious, agreeable'. Dims: Harmo, Harmon.

Haroldo Germanic *heri* 'army' + *wald* 'ruler, governor'. English: Harold.

Heberto see Heriberto

Héctor Greek *ekhein* 'to restrain, hold'. The name of a hero of the ancient Greek epic, the *Iliad*. Dims: Heco, Tito, Tocho. English: Hector.

Heladio, Hélido, Eladio From a Roman name, Helladius, derived from a Greek word meaning 'Greek'. San Eladio (Saint Helladius) was a 7th century archbishop of Tolédo, Spain. Feast February 18. Dims: Helio, Heladi. Fem: Hélida, Élida, Eladia, Heladia.

Heliodoro Greek *helios* 'sun' + *doron* 'gift'. Dims: Doro, Elio, Helio, Helito, Lolo.

Herardo see Erardo

Herberto see Heriberto

Hércules, Heraclio Latin Hercules, from Greek Herakles 'glory of the goddess Hera'. A hero of Greek myth. English: Hercules.

Heriberto, Herberto Germanic *heri* 'army' + *berht* 'shining, brilliant'. Dims: Berti, Berto, Beto, Heri. English: Herbert.

Hermán Germanic *heri* 'army' + *man* 'man'. English: Herman.

Hermelando, Hermelindo, Ermelando, Ermelindo Germanic *ermin* 'whole, entire' + *land* 'earth, country'. Fem: Hermelinda, Ermelinda.

Hermenegildo, Ermenegildo Germanic *ermin* 'whole, entire' + *hild* 'combat'. In the 6th century, Hermenegildo became the first Visigoth king to convert to Spain's Christian faith. Dims: Ermilo, Hermilo, Gildo. Fem: Hermenegilda.

Herminio, Erminio Germanic *ermin* 'entirely'. Fem: Erminia, Herminia.

Hernán, Hernando Variant forms of Fernán and Fernando. Dims: Nando, Nano. Fem: Hernanda.

Herón Greek *heros* 'hero'.

Hesiquio see Ezequiel

Higinio Greek *higinos* 'vigorous'. Dim: Ginio. Fem: Higinia.

Hilarino From a Roman clan name, Hilarinus, derived from Latin *hilaris* 'cheerful'. Fem: Hilarina.

Hilario, Hilarión From Latin *hilaris* 'cheerful'. San Hilario, who lived in France in the 4th century, is patron saint of backward children. Feast January 13. Dim: Lalo. Fem: Hilaria. English: Hilary, Hillary.

Hipólito Greek *hippos* 'horse' + *lytos* 'free, stampeding'. In Greek myth, the son of the hero Theseus and Hippolyta, the queen of the Amazons. Dims: Poli, Polo, Polito. Fem: Hipólita.

Hiram Hebrew 'my brother is exalted'. In the Old Testament, Hiram was king of Tyre in the time of David and Solomon. English: Hiram.

Homer, Omero From Greek *homeros* 'hostage'. Homer was the ancient Greek poet who composed the *Iliad* and the *Odyssey*. Diminutive: Mero. English: Homer.

Honesto Latin *honestus* 'honest, respectable'. Fem: Honesta.

Honorato Latin *honoratus* 'honored'. Fem: Honorata.

Honorio Latin *honorus* 'honorable'. Fem: Honoria, Honora.

Horacio From Horatius, name of one of the most distinguished Roman families. The name is Etruscan; its meaning is not known. Dim: Racho. English: Horatio, Horace.

Hoseá see Josué

Huáscar 'Gold chain' in the Quechua language. The name of the brother of Atahualpa, the last Inca ruler.

Huberto see Humberto

Hugo, Ugo, Hugón, Ugón Germanic *hug* 'mind, soul'. English: Hugo.

Hugolino Latinized form of Hugo.

Humberto, Huberto, Umberto Germanic *hum* 'giant' + *berht* 'shining, brilliant'. Dims: Berto, Beto, Tito. English: Hubert, Humbert.

Iago The medieval form of Jacob. Modern Spanish names derived from Iago are Diego, Jaime and Santiago.

Iban, Ibon Basque 'river valley'.

Ibero, Iberio, Ibérico, Iber From Latin *Hiberes* 'an inhabitant of Spain'.

Ibrán, Ibraín, Ibrahim Spanish names from the Arabic form of Abraham.

Ignacio Latin *ignatus* 'burning, ardent'. The Spanish saint, San Ignacio de Loyola (1492-1556) founded the Jesuit Order. Feast July 31. Dims: Joncho, Nacho, Nas. Catalan: Ignasi. Basque: Iñazio, Iñaki. Galician: Iñacio. Fem: Ignacia. English: Ignatius. Also see Iñigo.

Ildefonso Germanic *hild* 'combat' + *funs* 'prepared'. San Ildefonso was archbishop of Toledo, Spain, in the 7th century. Feast January 23. Dims: Joncho, Poncho.

Imanol Basque form of Manuel.

Iñazio, Iñaki Basque forms of Ignacio. Dim: Ñaki.

Indalecio Basque *inda* 'strength'. San Indalecio, a disciple of Santiago, is the patron saint of Almería, Spain. Feast May 15. Dim: Lecho. Basque: Indaleki.

Iñigo A Basque name, often used as the equivalent of Spanish Ignacio. Iñigo was the birth name of San Ignacio de Loyola (Saint Ignatius Loyola). Catalan: Inyigo.

Inocencio, Inocente Latin *innocens* 'innocent'. The name of thirteen popes. Dim: Chencho, Chente. Fem: Inocencia, Inocenta, Inocentia.

Ion A Basque form of Juan.

Ireneo Greek *eirene* 'peace'. Fem: Irene, Irenia.

Isaac, Isacio Hebrew 'he who laughs'. The son of Abraham and Sarah in the Old Testament. Basque: Ixaka. English: Isaac.

Isabelo, Isabelino Masculine forms of Isabel and Isabela, which originated as variants of the Biblical name, Elizabeth, 'God gives' in Hebrew.

Isaí, Jesé Hebrew 'God's grace'. In the Old Testament, the name of the father of David. English: Jesse.

Isaías, Isaio 'God is my salvation' in Hebrew. One of the great Old Testament prophets. English: Isaiah.

Isauro From the Latin name for an inhabitant of Isauria, a province in Asia Minor. Fem: Isaura.

Iscle Catalan form of Acisclo.

Isidoro, Isadoro Greek *Isis,* a goddess + *doron* 'gift' = 'gift of the goddess Isis'. Saint Isidore of Seville (ca 560-636), a renowned teacher and writer, is remembered on April 26. Because of his great intellectual achievements, he was named patron saint of computers and the Internet. Dims: Sidro, Doro. Fem: Isidora, Isadora. English: Isidore.

Isidro, Ysidro Greek Isis, a goddess + *doron* 'gift' = 'gift of the goddess Isis'. The 12th century San Isidro, patron saint of Madrid, is remembered on May 15. He is also the patron saint of farmers and laborers. Dims: Cedro, Chiro, Sidro. Fem: Isidra, Ysidra.

Ismael, Ysmael Hebrew 'God has heard'. Dim: Mel, Melito. English: Ishmael.

Israel Hebrew 'he who strives with God'. Dim: Isra.

Iván A Slavic cognate of Juan and John. Fem: Ivana. English: Ivan.

Ixaka Basque form of Isaac.

Jacinto Greek *hyakinthos* 'a dark lily'. Dim: Chinto, Jas. Fem: Jacinta.

Jacob, Jacobo Hebrew 'heel-grabber' or 'supplanter'. It was said that the biblical Jacob held onto his twin brother Esau's heel as he was born. Dim: Chago. Basque:

Jagoba, Fem: Jacoba, Jacobina. English: Jacob.

Jácome An older form of Jaime.

Jago see Iago

Jaime Modern form of Jacob, via Late Latin Iacomus. San Jaime (Saint James) is patron saint of the island of Formentera. Feast July 25. Dims: Jaimito, Jimmy, Mito. Catalan: Jaume. Basque: Jakes. Galician: Xaime. Feminine: Jacquelina, Jaquelina, Jaimita. English: James. See also Santiago, Diego.

Jair, Jairo Hebrew 'God will shine'.

Jandro, Jando Diminutives of Alejandro.

Jano A diminutive of Jenaro, Alejandro.

Jas A diminutive of Jacinto.

Jasón Derived from Iason, a Greek form of Joshua, a Hebrew name which means 'God is salvation'. Jason was a hero of Greek myth. English: Jason.

Jaume Catalan form of Jaime.

Javier see Xabier

Jenaro see Genaro

Jeraldo, Jerardo see Geraldo, Gerardo

Jeremías, Jeremío 'Appointed by God' in Hebrew. The name of an Old Testament prophet. English: Jeremiah, Jeremy.

Jericó Hebrew 'city of the moon'. A city destroyed by Joshua in the Bible.

Jermán, Jermano see **Germán**

Jerónimo, Gerónimo From the Greek name Hieronymus: *hieros* 'holy' + *onoma* 'name'. San Jéronimo (Saint Jerome) translated the Bible into Latin. He is the patron saint of students and librarians. Feast September 30. Dims: Chomo, Jero, Nono. English: Jerome.

Jerusalén Hebrew 'foundation of Sha-lem. Shalem was an early deity associated with the dawn.

Jesé see Isaí

Jesús From Ecclesiastic Greek Iesous, a form of Joshua, which means 'God is salvation' in Hebrew. Dims: Chu, Chuey, Chus, Chuy, Jesulito. Fem: Jesusa.

Jiméno A medieval form of Simeón. Catalan: Ximeno.

Joan Catalan form of Juan.

Joaquín Hebrew 'established by God'. According to popular tradition, this was the name of the father of the Virgin Mary (he is not mentioned in the Bible). Feast July 26. Diminutives: Juacho, Juaco, Juanco, Quin, Quino. Fem: Joaquina. Catalan: Joquím. Basque: Jokin, Yokim. Galician: Xaquím. English: Joachim.

Joel, Joelo Hebrew 'God is lord'. An Old Testament prophet. Fem: Joelda. English: Joel.

Jofre Catalan form of Godofredo.

Jokin Basque form of Joaquín.

Jon A Basque form of Juan.

Jonás, Jonaso Hebrew 'dove, pigeon'. English: Jonas, Jonah.

Jonatán Hebrew 'God has given'. Dim: Jon. English: Jonathan.

Joquím Catalan form of Joaquín. Dim: Quim.

Jordán 'Flowing downward' in Hebrew. The Jordan River flows from the Sea of Galilee to the Dead Sea. Fem: Jordana. English: Jordan.

Jordi Catalan form of Jorge. The patron saint of Catalunya, and a very popular name in that region.

Jorge Greek *georgos* 'farmer'. San Jorge (Saint George) is patron saint of Aragón, Spain, of Portugal and England, and also of soldiers and boy scouts. Feast April 23. Dims: Coco, Cocoy, Coque, Orito. Catalan: Jordi. Basque: Gorka, Jurgi. Fem: Georgia, Jorgelina. English: George.

José 'God makes great' in Hebrew. San José, the husband of the Virgin Mary, is remembered on March 19. He is patron saint of Mexico, of Peru, and also of carpenters, engineers and house hunters. Dims: Che, Chelín, Chepe, Chepo, Pepe, Pepín, Pepito. Fem: Josefa. Catalan: Josep, Bep (dim.). Basque: Joseba, Josepe. Galician: Xosé. English: Joseph. In 1999, José was the most popular name for baby boys in California and Texas, and the 28th most popular in the United States.

Josías Hebrew 'God heals'. In the Bible, a king of Judah. English: Josiah.

Josué, Joshé Hebrew 'God is salvation'. The successor of Moses, Joshua is the main character in the book of the Bible that bears his name. Dim: Josú. Variants are Hoseá and Oseás. English: Joshua.

Juacho, Juaco Diminutives of Joaquín.

Juan 'God is gracious' in Hebrew. San Juan Bautista (Saint John the Baptist) baptized Jesus in the Jordan River. Feast June 24. There have been 23 popes and more than 500 saints by this name. San Juan Evangelista (Saint John the Evangelist) is the patron saint of writers. Feast December 27. Dims: Chan, Chano, Jan, Johnny, Jon, Juano, Nito. Catalan: Joan. Basque: Ion, Jon, Joanes. Galician: Xoán. Fem: Juana. English: John.

Julián, Juliano From the Roman name Iulianus 'relative of Iulius'. San Julián is patron saint of travelers. Feast January 9.

Dim: Lián. Catalan: Julia. Basque: Julen. Fem: Juliana. English: Julian.

Julio From Iulius, a name borne by many famous Romans including Julius Caesar (ca 100-44 BC). Its meaning is unknown. Catalan: Juli. Basque: Yuli. Fem: Julia. English: Jules, Julius.

Juncho, Juincho Diminutives of Efraín.

Junipero Latin *iuniperus* 'juniper tree'. The Spanish form of the name of an Italian saint, Genebro, a disciple of Saint Francis of Assisi.

Jurgi Basque form of Jorge.

Justino From a Roman clan name, Iustinus, derived from Latin *iustus* 'righteous, just'. San Justino, an early martyr, is the patron saint of philosophers. Feast June 1. Fem: Justina. English: Justin.

Justo Latin *iustus* 'righteous, just'. Fem: Justa.

Juven, Juvencio Latin *iuventus* 'youth'. Fem: Juvencia.

Juvenal Latin *iuvenalis* 'young'. The name of a Roman writer and also of a 5th century saint.

Juventino, Juventín From a Roman clan name, Iuventinus, derived from Latin *iuventus* 'youth'. Fem: Juventina.

K Officially, there is no such letter in the Spanish language, though there is in Basque. Parents sometimes substitute 'k' for 'c' in baby names, usually girls' names such as Karla and Erika.

Kepa Basque form of Pedro.

Kerarta Basque form of Gerardo.

Kiki A diminutive of Enrique.

Kiko A diminutive of Eligio, Enrique and Federico.

Koldo Basque form of Luis.

Lacho A diminutive of Lázaro.

Ladislao Slavic *volod* 'rule, government' + *slav* 'glory'. Dims: Ladis, Lalo. Fem: Ladislada.

Lalo A diminutive of many names, including Eduardo and Geraldo.

Lando A diminutive of Orlando.

Lapo A diminutive of Serapio.

Laureano Latin *laureatus* 'crowned by laurels, victorious'. Fem: Laureana.

Laurencio An early form of Lorenzo, derived from the Latin name Laurens 'a native of Laurentium'. Laurentium, a port city south of Rome was named for the laurel trees that grew there. Fem: Laurencia. English: Lawrence, Laurence.

Laurentino From Laurentinus, a Roman name derived from Latin *laurus* 'laurel'. Dims: Lauro, Tino. Fem: Laurentina.

Laurindo Latin *laurus* 'laurel', signifying victory + the Germanic name-element *lind* 'sweet'. Fem: Laurinda.

Lauro Latin *laurus* 'laurel', signifying victory. Lauro is also a diminutive of Laurentino. Fem: Laura

Lautaro 'Swift bird' in the native Araucanian language of Chile and Argentina. The name of the hero of a 16th century epic, *La Araucana*, by the Chilean poet Alonso de Ercilla y Zúñiga. Dims: Lauro, Lauto.

Lázaro, Lazar Hebrew 'God, my help', the same origin as the name Eleazar. In the Bible, Lazarus was the man who raised from the dead by Jesus. Dims: Lacho, Laza. Catalan: Llàtzer. Basque: Elazar. Fem: Lázara. English: Lazarus.

Leandro Greek *leon* 'lion' + *andros* 'of man'. In Greek legend, Leander swam the treacherous Hellespont every night to visit Hero, his beloved. Leandro is also used as a diminutive of Alejandro. Dims: Lea, Andros. Catalan: Leandre. Basque: Lander.

Learco Greek *laos-archos* 'ruler of the city'.

Lejandro A diminutive of Alejandro.

Lelio From Laelius, the name of a Roman clan. Of Etruscan origin, its meaning is not know. Also a diminutive of Aurelio. Fem: Lelia.

Lencho A diminutive of Florencio.

Leó, León Latin *leo* or Greek *leon* 'lion'. There have been 13 popes by this name. Fem: Leona. English: Leo, Leon.

Leocadio Greek name for an inhabitant of Leukadia, an island in the Ionian Sea. Fem: Leocadia.

Leonardo A hybrid name from Greek *leon* 'lion' + Germanic *hard* 'strong, brave'. San Leonardo is patron saint of domestic animals. He is invoked against robbery. Dims: Leo, Nado, Nardo, Nayo. Fem: Leonarda. English: Leonard.

Leoncio Greek *leonteios* 'like a lion'. Dim: Loncho. Fem: Leoncia.

Leonilo, Leonel, Leonelo From a medieval French diminutive of León. Fem: Leonila. English: Lionel.

Leopardo Latin *leopardus* 'leopard'.

Leopoldo Germanic *liut* 'people' + *bald* 'bold, brave'. Dims: Polo, Polín. Fem: Leopolda. English: Leopold.

Leví Hebrew 'joined'. In the Old Testament, the name of the ancestor of the hereditary priests, the Levites. In the New Testament, the apostle Matthew was also known as Levi. Feminine: Levina. English: Levi.

Lián A diminutive of Julián.

Liberato, Liberado Latin *libero* 'to set free, to liberate'. A name from early Christian times that signified liberation from sin. Dims: Libe, Libro. Fem: Liberata.

Liborio Latin *libo* 'to make an offering to the gods'.

Libro A diminutive of Liberato.

Licerio Greek *lykerios* 'shining'. Catalan: Lleir.

Licho A diminutive of Eliseo, Lisandro and Ulises.

Lilo A diminutive of Baudilio, Cirilo and Virgilio.

Lin A diminutive of Antolín.

Lino Greek *linus* 'flax', an important plant in ancient times. It provided oil and linen cloth. In Greek myth, a man named Linus taught music to Hercules. Also a diminutive of men's names ending in '-lino', such as Catalino and Marcelino. Fem: Lina. English: Linus.

Lipe, Lipo Diminutives of Felipe.

Lisandro Greek *lysandros* 'liberator'. Lysander was a Spartan soldier and poet. Dims: Chando, Licho. Fem: Lisandra.

Lisardo, Lizardo see Elisardo

Lito Greek *litos* 'simple, easy'. Fem: Lita. Also a diminutive of names ending in '-l' or '-lo', such as Angelo and Cristobal.

Lleir Catalan form of Licerio.

Llejandro A diminutive of Alejandro.

Llop Catalan form of Lobo.

Llorenç Catalan form of Lorenzo.

Lluis Catalan form of Luis.

Lobo Spanish for 'wolf'. See also Lupo, Lope.

Locho A diminutive of Eulogio.

Lolo A diminutive of Eulogio, Lorenzo.

Lope Latin *lupus* 'wolf'. A very popular name in the Middle Ages and the source of the family name Lopez.

Lorenzo From a Roman name, Laurens, which meant 'a native of Laurentium' in Latin. Laurentium was a port city south of Rome. San Lorenzo, a 3rd century martyr, is the patron saint of Huesca, Spain. Feast August 10. Dims: Chencho, Lencho, Lolo, Renzo. Catalan: Llorenç. Fem: Lorenza. English: Lawrence.

Loyo A diminutive of Eulogio.

Lucas The Spanish name of the apostle Luke. It is probably the Greek form of the Roman name Lucius, from Latin *lux, lucis* 'light'. San Lucas is the patron saint of painters and sculptors. Feast October 18. Dims: Luc, Luca, Luco. Catalan: Lluc. Basque: Luka. Fem: Lucía. English: Luke.

Lucho A diminutive of Luis.

Luciano From a Roman name, Lucianus 'a relative of Lucius', derived from Latin *lux, lucis* 'light'. Dim: Chano. Fem: Luciana. English: Lucian.

Lucio From a popular Roman first name Lucius, derived from Latin *lux, lucis* 'light'. Fem: Lucía.

Ludovico Germanic *hlod* 'glory' + *wig* 'combat'. English: Ludwig.

Luis Germanic *hlod* 'glory' + *wig* 'combat'. Dim: Lucho. Catalan: Lluis. Basque: Aloxi, Koldo. Fem: Luisa. English: Louis.

Lulio, Lulo, Lulón From the family name of Ramón Lulio (Raymond Lully in English; Ramon Llull in his native Catalan), a medieval philosopher, mystic and poet. Feast June 29.

Lupo Latin *lupus* 'wolf'. See also Lobo, Lope.

Macario Greek *makaros* 'fortunate'. San Macario is patron saint of pastry chefs. There are 72 other saints by this name. Feast January 2. Fem: Macaria.

Macián, Macías see Matías

Magdaleno This is a masculine form of Magdalena, from the Bible name, María de Magdala (Mary Magdalen). Magdala was the name of a place in Galilee. Dims: Eleno, Maco.

Magín Latin *magnus* 'great'. San Magín is the patron saint of Tarragona, Spain. Feast August 19. Fem: Magina.

Mague A diminutive of Margarito.

Malaquías Hebrew 'messenger'. In the Bible, the name of the prophet who foretold the coming of the Messiah. Feast January 14. English: Malachi, Malachy.

Malco Greek *malakos* 'smooth, gentle'. The name of a Roman centurion healed by Jesus. Feast March 28.

Manasés, Manasio Hebrew 'causing to forget'. An Old Testament name borne by a son of Joseph and Asenath.

Manche A diminutive of Germán.

Mancho A diminutive of Maximiliano and Román.

Manco The name of the legendary first king of the Incas, Manco Capac.

Mando A diminutive of Armando.

Manel Catalan form of Manuel.

Manfredo Germanic *man* 'man' + *fridu* 'peace'.

Manoel Galician form of Manuel.

Manque 'Condor' in Araucanian, the language of the native Mapuche of Chile and Argentina.

Manrique Originally a diminutive of Amalarico, from Germanic *amal* 'work' + *ric* 'king'. Amalarico, a Visgoth king, sacked Rome in 5ᵗʰ century.

Manuel, Manuelo 'God is with us' in Hebrew. Dims: Huelo, Manel, Manelo, Manny, Mano, Manolo, Manu, Melo, Meño, Nelo. Catalan: Manel. Basque: Imanol. Fem: Manuela. English: Manuel. Emanuel, an older form of the name.

Marc Catalan form of Marcos.

Marçal Catalan form of Marcial. A popular name in Catalunya.

Marceliano, Marcelino From the Roman clan names Marcelianus and Marcelinus, Latin for 'a relative of Marcellus' (see Marcelo, below), Dims: Chelino, Lino. Fem: Marceliana.

Marcelo, Marcel From the Roman family name Marcellus (a diminutive of Marcus), from the name of the Roman god of war, Mars. Dims: Chelo, Lino. Fem: Marcela. English: Marcel.

Marcial Latin *martialis* 'sacred to the god Mars'. Catalan: Marçal.

Marciano From the Roman name Marcianus 'a relative of Marcius' (see Marcio, below). Dim: Chano. Fem: Marciana.

Marcio From the Roman clan name Marcius, derived from the name of the god of war, Mars. Fem: Marcia.

Marcos, Marco From the Roman name Marcus, derived from Mars, god of war.

San Marcos (Saint Mark) was an apostle and evangelist. Feast September 27. Catalan: Marc. Basque: Marka. Fem: Marcia, Marquesa. English: Mark, Marcus.

Margarito Latin *margarita* 'pearl'. Dims: Mague, Rito. Fem: Margarita.

María From Miriam, a Hebrew name of uncertain meaning—perhaps 'bitter' or 'grieved' or 'rebellion'. Given to boys as a second or middle name, José María, for example.

Mariano Latin 'a relative of Marius', this name can also signify devotion to the Virgin Mary. It is a popular name in the Philippines. Fem: Mariana.

Marín, Marino Latin *marinus* 'of the sea'. The name of two popes. Fem: Marina.

Mario From a Roman clan name, Marius. Dim: Mayito. English: Mario.

Marón Latin *maris* 'sea'.

Martín, Martino From a Roman name, Martinus, derived from the name of the god of war, Mars. The 4ᵗʰ century San Martín (Saint Martin) of Tours, France, is patron saint of that country, and also of horses, riders and winemakers. Feast November 11. San Martín de Porres of Peru (1579-1639) is patron saint of television and of people of mixed race. Feast November 5. Diminutives: Marti, Tin. Catalan: Martí. Basque: Mattin, Matxin. Fem: Matina. English: Martin.

Martiniano From the Roman name, Martinianus ('a relative of Martinus' in Latin) from the name of the god of war, Mars. Fem: Martiniana.

Mateo Hebrew 'gift of God'. The apostle San Mateo (Saint Matthew) was once a Roman tax collector, and is the patron saint of bankers and accountants. Feast

September 21. Dims: Matty, Teo. Catalan: Mateu. English: Matthew.

Matías, Mateos New Testament Greek form of Matthew, 'gift of God' in Hebrew. The name of the apostle who was chosen to replace Judas. Feast February 24. English: Matthias.

Mattin, Matxin Basque forms of Martín.

Mauricio From the Roman name Mauritius, derived from Latin *maurus* 'a Moor, a person from North Africa'. San Mauricio is patron saint of weavers and dyers. Feast September 22. Dims: Maure, Richo. Fem: Mauricia. English: Maurice.

Maurilio, Maurilo Latin diminutive of *maurus* 'a Moor, a person from North Africa'.

Mauro, Maureo, Maurón Latin *maurus* 'a Moor, a person from North Africa'. Fem: Maura, Mora.

Maximiliano From Maximilianus, Latin for 'a relative of Maximus'. San Maximiliano, a Roman soldier, is patron saint of conscientious objectors. Feast March 12. Dims: Chilano, Mancho. Fem: Maximiliana. English: Maximilian.

Maximino, Maximiano Latin 'a relative of Maximo' (see Máximo, below). Fem: Maximiana. Dims: Max, Maxi, Mino.

Máximo Latin *maximus* 'greatest, best'. Dims: Max, Maxi.

Mecho A diminutive of Nemesio.

Medardo Germanic *maht* 'force' + *hard* 'strong, brave'. San Medardo is protector of vineyards. Feast June 8.

Mel A diminutive of Amelio, Melchor, Samuel and other 'mel' names.

Melanio Greek *melos* 'black'. Feminine: Melania.

Melchor Persian *melk* 'king' + *quart* 'city'. According to medieval popular tradition, Melchior was the name of one of the three Magi who carried gifts to the Christ Child. Feast January 6. Dim: Mel.

Melitón, Melito Latin *mellitus* 'sweet as honey'. Fem: Melina, Melida.

Melo, Melito Diminutives of Emilio, Ismael and Manuel.

Melquíades Hebrew 'king of righteousness'. The name of a 4th century pope (Miltiades in English). Dim: Mequila.

Memo A diminutive of Guillermo.

Meno A diminutive of Filomeno.

Meño A diminutive of Manuel.

Mente A diminutive of Clemente.

Merco A diminutive of Américo.

Mercurio Latin *merx* 'business' + *cura* 'care'. Mercurius (Mercury in English) was the messenger of the Roman gods and the patron of both merchants and thieves.

Mero A diminutive of Homero and Baldomero.

Micho A diminutive of Benjamín.

Miguel 'Who is like God?' in Hebrew. An archangel, the leader of the heavenly host, Michael was also proclaimed a preChristian saint. San Miguel is patron saint of paratroopers, radiologists and supermarket workers. Feast September 29. Dims: Lito, Mico, Mique, Miqui. Catalan: Miquel. Basque: Mikel. Fem: Micaela. English: Michael.

Millán Originally a diminutive of Emiliano. A name given in honor of the 6th century Spanish saint, Millán de Cogulla. Feast November 12.

Milo A diminutive of Emilio, Carmelo.

Min, Mincho Diminutives of Fermín.

Mingo A diminutive of Domingo.

Mino A diminutive of Guillermo.

Mique, Miqui Diminutives of Miguel.

Miquel Catalan form of Miguel.

Miro A diminutive of Casimiro.

Miró, Mirón Greek *myron* 'myrrh'. Fem: Mira.

Modesto Latin *modestus* 'moderate, modest'. Fem: Modesta.

Moisés The origin and meaning of this biblical name are not known. It could be Egyptian rather than Hebrew. In the Old Testament, Moses led the Israelites out of Egypt. Dims: Moi, Monche, Monchi.

Mon A diminutive of Salomón and Solomón.

Mon, Mongo Diminutives of Ramón.

Monche, Monchi Diminutives of Moisés.

Monchi, Monchín Diminutives of Raimundo.

Moncho A diminutive of Raimundo and Simón.

Mongo A diminutive of Raimundo and Ramón

Moñi A diminutive of Salomón and Solomón.

Moño A diminutive of Ramón

Montano Latin *montanus* 'of the mountains' or 'mountaineer'. Fem: Montana.

Monte, Montes, Montez Latin *montis* 'of the mountains'.

Mundo A diminutive of Raimundo and Segismundo.

Nacho A diminutive of Anastasio, Ignacio and Narciso.

Nahuel 'Tiger' in the Araucanian language of the native Mapuche of Chile and Argentina.

Nahum, Naún Hebrew 'God comforts'. The name of an Old Testament prophet. English: Nehemiah.

Naldo, Nalo Diminutives of Arnoldo, Reinaldo and Reginaldo.

Nancho A diminutive of Venancio.

Nando, Nano Diminutives of Fernando and Fernán.

Nano A diminutive of Viviano.

Naphtalí see Neftalí

Napoleón Italian *Napoli* 'Naples'. The name of a 4th century martyr saint, as well as the famous (or infamous) French general. Dims: Napolo, León.

Narciso Greek Narkissos, from *narkor* 'to put to sleep'. In myth, a young man who fell in love with his own reflection. San Narciso, patron of Girona, Spain, lived 116 years. Feast October 29. Dims: Chicho, Chico, Nacho, Narsi. Catalan: Narcís. Basque: Narkio. Fem: Narcisa.

Nardo A diminutive of Leonardo.

Nas A diminutive of Ignacio.

Natal, Natalio Latin *Natalis* 'Christmas'. Fem: Natalia.

Natán, Natanael, Nataniel Hebrew 'God has given'. The name of a prophet in the court of King David. English: Nathan, Nathaniel.

Nato A diminutive of Donato.

Navarro Basque *nava* 'a plain between mountains'.

Nayo A diminutive of Leonardo.

Nazar, Nazario, Názaro 'Set apart, consecrated' in Hebrew. Fem: Nazaria.

Nazareno Hebrew 'a person from Nazareth [Jesus' birthplace]'. Dim: Nazar.

Necho A diminutive of Ernesto.

Neftalí, Naftalí Hebrew, 'wrestling, battle'. English: Naphtali.

Nelo A diminutive of Cornelio, Daniel and Manuel.

Nelson Old Irish *nél* 'cloud' + the English patronmyic, son. A popular first name in Latin America.

Nemesio From Nemesis, Roman goddess of justice, who punished pride and arrogance. Dim: Mecho. Fem: Nemesia.

Nereo Greek Nereus, god of the sea. Fem: Nerea.

Neri, Nery From the family name of the Italian saint, Felipe Nery. Feast May 26.

Nesti A diminutive of Ernesto.

Néstor The Greek name of a hero of the Trojan war. The origin and meaning of the name are not known.

Nicanor, Nicandro Greek *nike* 'victory' + *aner, andros* 'of man'. A popular name among early Christians. Dim: Nico. Fem: Nicanora.

Nicasio Greek *nikasios* 'victorious'. Dim: Nica.

Niceto Greek *niketas* 'victor'.

Nicho, Nisio Diminutives of Dionisio.

Nico A diminutive of 'Nic-' names.

Nicolás, Nicolao Greco-Latin *nike* 'victory' + *laus* 'praise'. San Nicolás, a 4th century bishop (also known in the U.S. as Santa Claus) is protector of children and patron saint of Greece and Russia, and of Alicante, Spain. Feast December 6. Diminutives: Cola, Colas, Lacho, Nico. Catalan: Nicolau. Basque: Nikola. Fem: Nicolasa. English: Nicholas.

Nil, Nilo Popular Catalan names, from Latin *Nilus* 'Nile river'. They are also diminutives of Danilo.

Nino A diminutive of names ending in '-nino'.

Noé Hebrew 'to rest, to comfort'. In the Old Testament, Noah built the Ark and survived the great flood. English: Noah.

Noel, Noelino The Spanish form of a French name meaning Christmas, equivalent of Spanish Navidad. Feast December 25. Fem: Noelia. English: Noel.

Nolasco From the family name of San Pedro de Nolasco, who witnessed an apparition of the Virgin Mary in 1218. He founded the Mercedarian Order. Feast May 13.

Nono A diminutive of Jerónimo.

Norberto Germanic *nord* 'north' + *berht* 'shining, brilliant'. Dim: Berto.

Normán, Normando, Normano Germanic *nord* 'north' + *man* 'man'. Fem: Norma. English: Norman.

Nosito A diminutive of Donoso.

Nulfo A diminutive of Arnulfo.

Nuncio Latin *nuntio* 'to announce'. Fem: Nuncia.

Oberto see Alberto

Octaviano From the Roman name Octavianus 'a relative of Octavius', derived from Latin *octavus* 'eighth'. Dim: Tano. Fem: Octaviana.

Octavio, Octavo From the Roman clan name Octavius, derived from Latin *octavus* 'eighth'. Dims: Tavo, Tavio. Fem: Octavia. English: Octavius.

Odilón Germanic *odo* 'wealth'. Fem: Odila, Odilia.

Olav, Olavo A Viking name that meant 'ancestor' in Old Norse. English: Olaf.

Oleguer, Olegario Germanic *adal* 'noble' + *gar* 'spear'. San Oleguer was bishop of Barcelona in the 12th century. Feast March 6. Dim: Olich.

Olimpio Greek Olympos, the name of the site of the Olympic games and also of the mountain home of the Greek gods. Fem: Olimpia.

Oliver, Oliverio, Oliverios, Olivero, Oliviero Spanish versions of Olivier, a fictional hero of medieval French romance. The names may be derived from Latin *olivarius* 'olive tree' or from the Norse name, Olaf. English: Oliver.

Omar, Omaro A popular Arabic name mentioned in the Bible. It means 'talkative' in Hebrew. Fem: Omara.

Onésimo Greek *onesimos* 'useful'.

Onofre Germanic *un* 'give' + *fridu* 'peace'. San Onofre is patron of weavers. Feast June 12. English: Humphrey.

Orencio Latin *oriens* 'rising sun', a name for a person from the east.

Orestes, Oreste Greek *oros* 'mountains'. The name of a character from Greek myth, the son of Agamemnon.

Orio A diminutive of Gregorio.

Oriol After the last name of a 17th century saint, San José Oriol of Barcelona. A popular name in Catalunya.

Orito A diminutive of Jorge.

Orlán, Orlando Variants of the name Rolando, from Germanic *hrod* 'glorious' + *land* 'earth, country'. Dims: Lando, Lalo. English: Orlando.

Orosco Basque *oros* 'holly tree'. A surname also used as a first name.

Óscar Anglo-Saxon *Ans*, a god name + *gar* 'spear'. Dim: Osqui. English: Oscar.

Oseás see Josué

Osías see Azario

Osmundo Germanic *ost* 'east' + *mund* 'protection'.

Osqui A diminutive of Oscar.

Osvaldo, Oswaldo Germanic *ost* 'east' + *wald* 'ruler'. Dims: Valdo, Waldo. English: Oswald, Waldo.

Otilio Germanic *othal* 'fatherland'. Dims: Tilo, Tilio. Fem: Otilia.

Oto, Otón Germanic *odo* 'wealth'. English: Otto.

Ozías see Azario

Pablo, Paulo, Paúl Latin *paulus* 'small'. The apostle San Pablo (Saint Paul) was the most important missionary of early Christianity. He is patron saint of missionaries, tentmakers and saddlers. Feast June 29. Dims: Lino, Pauli, Polín. Catalan: Pau. Basque: Paul, Pol. Fem: Paula, Paola, Pabla, Pablita. English: Paul.

Paciano Latin *pax, pacis* 'peace'. San Paciano was a bishop of Barcelona in the 4th century. Catalan: Pacià.

Paciente Latin *patientia* 'patience, endurance'. Fem: Paciencia.

Pacífico Latin *pacificus* 'peaceful'. A popular name in the Philippines. Dim: Paco.

Paco A diminutive of Francisco, Pacifico and Pascual.

Pacomio Greek *pakomios* 'having broad shoulders'.

Palmiro Latin *palma* 'palm'. The name originally signified that a person had brought back a palm leaf from the Holy Land. Fem: Palmira, Palmir, Palma.

Palomo Latin *palumbes* 'a dove'. Fem: Paloma.

Pancho A diminutive of Francisco.

Pancracio Greek *pan* 'all, complete' + *kration* 'force, strength'.

Pánfilo Greek *pan* 'all, complete' + *philos* 'friend'.

París The origin of this name is not certain. It was borne by a hero of the Trojan War and also by a 3rd century saint remembered on August 5.

Parmenio, Parmeno Greek *parameno* 'faithful'.

Pascual, Pascal Latin *paschalis* (from Hebrew *pesach* 'Passover') an adjective meaning 'relating to Easter'. Dims: Paco, Pasco. Fem: Pascua, Pascualina.

Pastor Latin *pastor* 'shepherd'. An early Christian name which refers to Christ as El Buen Pastor, the Good Shepherd. Fem: Pastora.

Patricio Latin *patricius* 'aristocrat'. This name was adopted by the 5th century Celtic missionary who became patron saint of Ireland. Feast March 17. Dims: Pachi, Pat, Richo, Ticho. Fem: Patricia. English: Patrick.

Pau Catalan form of Pablo and a popular name in Catalunya.

Paúl, Paulo see Pablo

Paulino From the Roman name Paulinus 'a relative of Paulus', derived from Latin *paulus* 'small'. Fem: Paulina.

Pavi Basque form of Fabio.

Payo A diminutive of Pelayo.

Paz Spanish for 'peace' and a Marian name, in honor of Nuestra Señora de la Paz (Our Lady of Peace). Given to boys as the second or middle name 'de la Paz'.

Pedro Latin *petrus* 'rock'. A perennially popular name. In the Bible, Jesus gave this name to Simon, son of Jonas, saying, 'Thou art Peter, and upon this rock I will build my church'. Feast June 29. San Pedro de Alcantara, a 16th century writer and mystic, is the patron saint of Brazil and of Estremadura, Spain. Dims: Pedri, Pedrín, Pedrio, Pepe, Perico, Pico, Piero. Catalan: Pere. Basque: Pello, Kepa. Fem: Petra. English: Peter.

Pelayo, Pelagio Greek *pelagos* 'deep sea'. San Pelayo is the patron saint of those who are abandoned. Feast June 26. Dim: Payo.

Peli Basque form of Félix.

Pello Basque form of Pedro.

Pepe A diminutive of Felipe, Juan, José and Pedro.

Pere Catalan form of Pedro.

Peregrino Latin *peregrinus* 'pilgrim'.

Perfecto Latin *perfectus* 'complete, perfect'. Fem: Perfecta.

Perico A diminutive of Pedro.

Perrando Basque form of Fernando.

Perseo A name from Greek myth, of unknown origin. Perseus slew the monster Gorgon.

Pico A diminutive of Pedro.

Pifano A diminutive of Epifanio.

Pilo, Piyo Diminutives of Porfirio.

Pino A diminutive of Agripino and Crispino.

Pío Latin *pius* 'pious, dutiful'. The name of 12 popes. Fem: Pía.

Pirro Greek 'red hair'.

Plácido, Placid Latin *placidus* 'gentle, quiet'. Dims: Plací, Plasio. Fem: Placida.

Platón Greek *platon* 'wide-shouldered'. The name of the great philosopher of Ancient Greece, Plato.

Pol The Catalan form of Pablo. A popular name in Catalunya.

Poli, Polo, Polito Diminutives of Apolo, Leopoldo, Hipolito and Pablo.

Polín A diminutive of Pablo.

Pompeyo From the Roman clan name, Pompeius, from Latin *pompa* 'procession'.

Ponce, Poncio From a Roman clan name, Pontius. Its meaning is not known.

Poncho A diminutive of Alfonso and Ildefonso.

Ponciano From the Roman name Pontianus 'relative of Pontius'. Dim: Chano. Fem: Ponciana.

Porfirio Greek *porphyrion* 'dressed in purple [a color associated with royalty]'.

Prantxes Basque form of Francisco.

Práxedes Greek 'firm of purpose'. The name of a 2nd century saint who gave his wealth to the poor.

Primitivo Latin *primitus* 'original'. The name of several early Spanish saints. Dim: Primeto.

Primo, Primeiro Latin *primus* 'first'. A name given to first-born children. Fem: Prima, Primeira.

Prisciliano Latin *priscus* 'old, venerable'. San Prisciliano, a first century saint, was a convert of Saint Peter. Feast January 14. Dims: Chano, Chiano.

Priscilo A Latin diminutive of *priscus* 'ancient, venerable'. Fem: Priscila.

Prisco Latin *priscus* 'ancient, venerable'.

Próspero Latin *prosperus* 'lucky'.

Prudencio, Prudente Latin *prudentia* 'prudence, knowledge (especially knowledge of the future)'. San Prudencio, who lived in the 8th century, was a bishop of Tarazona, Spain. Dims: Prudo, Prudón. Fem: Prudencia.

Quelo A diminutive of Ezequiel.

Queño A diminutive of Eugenio.

Querubín Hebrew 'angel'.

Quico A diminutive of Enrique and Federico.

Quilino A diminutive of Tranquilino.

Quilo A diminutive of Aquileo, Aquiles and Tranquilo.

Quim A diminutive of Joquím, Catalan form of Joaquín.

Quin A diminutive of Joaquín and of names beginning with 'Quin-'.

Quintiliano From the Roman name Quintilianus, 'a relative of Quintilis'. Dim: Quin.

Quintilo From the Roman name Quintilis, derived from Latin *quintius* 'fifth'. Dim: Quin.

Quintín From the Roman name Quintinus, derived from Latin *quintius* 'fifth'.

Dim: Quin. Fem: Quintina. English: Quentin.

Quinto From the Roman name Quintius 'fifth'. Dim: Quin. Fem: Quinta.

Quique A diminutive of Enrique and Ricardo.

Quirino Latin Quirinus. This is another name for Romulus, legendary founder of Rome. From *quiris,* a Sabine word meaning 'spear'. Fem: Quirina.

Quirze, Quiríaco, Ciríaco Greek *kyrios* 'master'. San Quirze (Saint Cyriack) was an infant martyr. Dims: Siria, Yaco. Fem: Ciríaca.

Quito A diminutive of Francisco.

Racho A diminutive of Horacio.

Rafael 'God has healed' in Hebrew. The name of one of three archangels mentioned in the Old Testament, all of whom were made Christian saints. Dims: Fafa, Falo, Fallo, Felo, Rafa, Rafe. Fem: Rafaela. English: Raphael.

Raimundo Germanic *rad* 'counsel, advice' + *mund* 'protector'. An older form of Ramón. Feast January 7. Dims: Monchi, Monchín, Moncho, Mongo, Mundo, Rai, Ray. Catalan: Raimon. Fem: Raimunda. English: Raymond.

Rainero, Rainerio Germanic *rad* 'counsel, advice' + *heri* 'army'. Dims: Rai, Ray. English: Rayner.

Ramiro Germanic *rad* 'counsel, advice' + *miru* 'protector'. Ramiro II of León defeated the Muslims in 950. He is patron saint of León. Catalan: Ramir. Basque: Erramir. Fem: Ramira.

Ramón, Raimón Germanic *rad* 'advice, counsel' + *mund* 'protector'. A Catalan form of Raimundo. San Ramón Nonato,

a 12th century saint of Catalunya, is a patron of pregnant women and midwives. Feast August 31. Dims: Mon, Mongo, Moño, Monxo. Fem: Ramona. Basque: Erramun. English: Ramon.

Randolfo, Ranulfo Germanic *rand* 'a shield' + *wulf* 'wolf'. Dim: Rando. English: Randolph, Ralph.

Raúl, Raulo Germanic *rad* 'counsel, advice' + *wulf* 'wolf'. Dims: Roy, Rulo. English: Raoul.

Refugio Spanish for 'refuge'. A name bestowed in honor of the Virgin Mary as Nuestra Señora de Refugio (Our Lady of Refuge). Feast August 13. Dims: Cuco, Fucho, Fujo. Fem: Refugia.

Regis Latin *rex, regis* 'king'. Fem: Regina.

Reinaldo, Renaldo, Reginaldo Germanic *ragin* 'counsel, advice' + *wald* 'ruler, governor'. Dims: Ray, Rey, Naldo, Nalo. Fem: Reinalda, Renalda. English: Reynold, Reginald.

Remigio Latin *remex, remigis* 'oarsman'. Dims: Mich, Remo.

Remo Latin *remus* 'oar'. The legendary hero, Remus, was twin brother of Romulus, founder of the city of Rome. Remo is also a diminutive of Remigio. English: Remus.

Renato Latin *renato* 'reborn'. René, the French form of the name, is also used. Fem: Renata.

Renzo A diminutive of Lorenzo.

Reubén see Rubén

Reyes, Reies Spanish for 'kings'. A name given in honor of the three kings who carried gifts to the Christ Child. La Adoración de los Reyes (the Feast of the Epiphany) January 6. Dim: Rey.

Riberto see Rigoberto

Ricardo, Ricario Germanic *ric* 'king' + *hard* 'strong, brave'. Dims: Cardo, Cayo, Riche, Ricky, Rico. Catalan: Ricard, Ricari. Basque: Errikarta. Fem: Ricarda, Ricaria. English: Richard.

Richo A diminutive of Patricio.

Rico A diminutive of Ricardo and other 'ric' names.

Rigoberto, Riberto Germanic *ric* 'king' + *berht* 'shining, brilliant'. Dims: Beto, Bert, Rigo. Fem: Rigoberta.

Rinaldo see Reinaldo

Rio Spanish for 'river'. A recent name.

Rito A diminutive of Margarito.

Robertino Germanic *hrod* 'glorious' + *berht* 'shining, brilliant', with a Latin name ending.

Roberto Germanic *hrod* 'glorious' + *berht* 'shining, brilliant'. Dims: Berto, Beto. Catalan: Robert. Basque: Erroberta. Fem: Roberta. English: Robert.

Roc Catalan form of Roque.

Rode Germanic *hrod* 'glorious'.

Rodi A diminutive of Rodrigo.

Rodolfo, Rodulfo Germanic *hrod* 'glorious' + *wulf* 'wolf'. Dims: Rolo, Rudi, Rudo, Rulo. English: Rolf.

Rodrigo Germanic *hrod* 'glorious' + *ric* 'king'. The 11th century hero Rodrigo Díaz de Bivar was the inspiration for the Spanish national epic, *Cantar de mio Cid.* Dims: Gigo, Igo, Rodi, Roy. Fem: Rodriga. English: Roderick.

Rogelio, Rogerio Germanic *hrod* 'glorious' + *gar* 'spear'. Dims: Gela, Geyo, Roger. English: Roger.

Roldán, Rolando Germanic: *hrod* 'glorious' + *land* 'earth, country'. Variants of the French name Roland. Roland was the hero of *Le Chanson de Roland,* an 11th century romance of chivalry. Dims: Olo, Orlo, Lando. Fem: Rolanda, Roldana. English: Roland. Also see Orlando.

Rolo A diminutive of Rodolfo.

Román, Roman, Romano Latin *Romanus* 'a Roman'. Dim: Mancho. Fem: Romana. English: Roman.

Romeo A name for a person who made a pilgrimage to Rome. Fem: Romea.

Romualdo Germanic *hrod* 'glorious' + *wald* 'ruler, governor'.

Rómulo From the Latin name Romulus. According to legend, Romulus founded the city of Rome. The origin and meaning of the name are not known.

Roque, Rocco Germanic *hroc* 'shout'. The Paraguayan saint, Roque Gonzales de Santa Cruz (1576-1628) is remembered November 17. Catalan: Roc. Fem: Roquelia.

Rosalindo, Rosalino Germanic *hros* 'horse' + *lind* 'sweet, pleasing'. Fem: Rosalindo, Rosalina.

Rosalío Latin *Rosalias,* the name of a festival in which roses were placed upon the tombs of the dead. Fem: Rosalía.

Rosario Spanish for 'rosary'. A name bestowed in honor of the Virgin Mary as Nuestra Señora del Rosario (Our Lady of the Rosary). Feast October 7. Often part of the middle name, 'del Rosario'.

Rosendo Germanic *hrod* 'glory' + *sind* 'path'. San Rosendo was a 10th century saint of Galicia, Spain. Dim: Chendo. Fem: Rosenda.

Roy A diminutive of Raúl and Rodrigo.

Rubén, Reubén 'Behold, a son' in Hebrew. In the Bible, the name of the first son of Jacob and Leah. Dim: Rube. English: Reuben, Ruben.

Rudolfo see Rodolfo

Rufino From the Roman clan name Rufinus, derived from Latin *rufus* 'ruddy, red'. Fem: Rufina.

Rufo, Rufio From Latin *rufus* 'ruddy, red'. English: Rufus.

Rulo A diminutive of Raúl and Rudolfo.

Ruperto An early form of the name Roberto, from Germanic *hrod* 'glorious' + *berht* 'shining, brilliant'. Dim: Rupo. English: Rupert.

Ruy Germanic *hrod* 'glorious'. Ruy is also a diminutive of Raúl and Rodrigo.

Sabas Hebrew 'sabbath'. Dim: Sabitas.

Sabino Latin *Sabinus* 'a Sabine'. The Sabines were an ancient tribe of Italy, rivals of the Romans. Fem: Sabina.

Sadurní Catalan form of Saturnino.

Salomón, Solomón Hebrew 'peaceful'. The name of a king of Israel renowned for his wisdom. Dims: Mon, Moñi, Sol. English: Solomon.

Salvador Late Latin *salvator* 'savior', a name first used by early Christians in honor of Jesus Christ. Dims: Sal, Chava. Basque: Gaizka. Fem: Salvadora.

Salvio, Salvo, Salvino, Salviano Latin *salvare* 'to save'. Dim: Sal.

Samuel 'God has listened' in Hebrew. Samuel was an Old Testament judge and prophet. Diminutives: Sam, Sammy. English: Samuel.

Sancho Latin *sancio* 'to consecrate, to make sacred'. A royal name in Castille, León and Navarre. Also the name of a character in *Don Quixote* by Miguel de Cervantes. Catalan: Sanç. Basque: Deunoro. Fem: Sancha, Sainza.

Sándalo, Sandalio Germanic *sand* 'true' + *wulf* 'wolf'. San Sándalo was a 9th century martyr saint of Córdoba, Spain, and is patron of that city. Feast September 3.

Sandro Originally a diminutive of Alejandro. Dims: Sando, Sandito.

Sansón Hebrew 'child of Shamash [an early sun god]'. In the Bible, Samson was the champion of the Israelites against the Philistines. A saint by this same name, San Sansón, was an early missionary in France. Feast July 28. English: Samson.

Santiago The Spanish name of Saint James the Apostle, whose Latin name was Jacob. By the Middle Ages, Jacob had become Iago in Spanish, and then Sant Iago was condensed into Santiago. According to popular tradition, Santiago evangelized Spain and died at Compostela, a site that became one of the most important destinations of religious pilgrims in the Middle Ages. Santiago is the patron saint of Spain and Chile. Feast July 25. Dims: Chago, Chango, Chanti, Santi, Yago. Basque: Santi, Xanti. See also: Jaime, Diego.

Santito A diminutive of Crisanto and Santos.

Santos, Santo, Santino, Santón Latin *sanctus* 'sacred'. Fem: Santina.

Sarito A diminutive of César.

Saturnino Latin Saturnus, the Roman god of agriculture and civilization. The

3rd century San Saturnino is patron saint of Pamplona, Spain. Feast November 29. Diminutives: Nino, Saturni, Tuno. Catalan: Sadurni.

Saúl, Saulo 'Desired' in Hebrew. In the New Testament, Saul was the original name of the apostle Paul. Feast October 20. Fem: Saula. English: Saul.

Sebastián, Sebastiano Greek *sebastos* 'honored'. San Sebastián, a Roman soldier and martyr, is patron saint of soldiers, athletes and archers. Feast January 20. Dims: Bastián, Chano, Chebo, Sebo. Fem: Sebastiana. English: Sebastian.

Segismundo Germanic *sigi* 'victorious' + *mund* 'protector'. Dims: Mundo, Muno. Fem: Segismunda. English: Sigmund.

Segundo, Segundino Latin *secundus* 'second', a name given to a second-born son. Fem: Segunda.

Sequel A diminutive of Ezequiel.

Serafín, Serafino 'Burning ones, angels' in Hebrew. Dim: Serafito. Fem: Serafina.

Serapio, Serapion Greek *serapeion* 'a temple'. Dim: Lapo.

Sergio From a Roman clan name, Sergius. The meaning of the name is not known.

Servando Latin *servandus* 'observing'. The 3rd century saint, San Servando is patron of Cádiz, Spain. Feast October 23.

Severino, Severiano From the Roman name Severinus 'related to Severus', derived from Latin *severus* 'strict, stern'. Dim: Seve. Fem: Severina.

Severo From a Roman family name, Severus, derived from Latin *severus* 'strict, stern'. San Severo was a 7th century bishop of Barcelona, Spain. Feast November 6. Dim: Seve.

Sidonio Latin 'a native of Sidon [a city in Phoenicia, now Lebanon]'. Dims: Sidio, Sido. Fem: Sidonia. English: Sidney.

Sidro A diminutive of Isidoro and Isidro.

Sigfrido, Sigifredo Germanic *sigi* 'victory' + *fridu* 'peace'.

Silvano Latin *silvanus* 'a forest-dweller'. The name of the Roman god of the forest. Fem: Silvana.

Silverio Latin *silva* 'woods'. Fem: Silveria.

Silvestre, Silvestro Latin *silvester* 'a person who lives in the forest'. Dims: Veche, Veto. English: Sylvester.

Silvino From a Roman name, Silvinus, from Latin *silva* 'woods'. Dim: Vino.

Silvio Latin *silva* 'woods'. Silvius was a son of Aeneas, legendary founder of the city of Rome. Dim: Chivi. Fem: Silvia.

Simeón Hebrew 'God hears me'. In the Bible, Simeon blessed the baby Jesus in the temple. Feast February 18.

Simón, Simon New Testament Greek form of Simeon, Hebrew for 'God hears me'. Many Simons are mentioned in the New Testament, but the popularity of Simon as a first name is due to devotion to the apostle Simon Peter. Feast October 28. Dim: Moncho. Catalan: Simó. Basque: Ximun. Fem: Simona. English: Simon.

Sinforoso Greek *symphora* 'companion'. Dims: Bocho, Foro. Fem: Sinforosa.

Siri A diminutive of Ciríaco.

Siro Latin *Sirius* 'a Syrian'. Fem: Sira.

Sol A diminutive of Solomón.

Solano Latin *solana* 'a sunny place'. A name given in honor of San Francisco Solano (1549-1610), a missionary to Peru. Feast July 14. Fem: Solana.

Solomón see Salomón

Sotero Greek *soter* 'savior'. Dims: Sotes, Soto. Fem: Sotera.

Stancio, Stanzo Diminutives of Constancio.

Stefano see Esteban

Tacho A diminutive of Anastasio.

Taciano Latin Tatianus 'a relative of Tatius' (see Tacio, below).

Tacio, Tación Latin Tatius, the name of the legendary king of the Sabines in the time of Romulus. The meaning of the name is not known. Fem: Tacia, Tatiana.

Tadeo This name probably has the same source as Teodoro: Greek *theos* 'God' + *doron* 'gift' = 'gift of God'. Dim: Tadi. English: Thaddeus.

Tajo A diminutive of Eustaquio.

Tanas, Tani Diminutives of Estanislao.

Tancredo Germanic *thank* 'thought' + *rad* 'advice, counsel'. The name of a hero of the Crusades, celebrated in *Jerusalem Liberated* by Italian poet Torquato Tasso.

Tano A diminutive of Octaviano and other names that end in '-an' and '-ano'.

Tasio A diminutive of Anastasio.

Taurio, Taurión, Taurino Latin *taurus* 'bull'. Dims: Tauro, Toro.

Tavín, Tavo Diminutives of Gustavo.

Tavo, Tavio Diminutives of Octavio.

Tebe A diminutive of Esteban.

Techo A diminutive of Tereso.

Telésforo Greek *telesphoron* 'messenger'.

Telmo, Elmo Germanic *helm* 'protector'. The medieval saint's name, Sant Elmus, evolved into two separate names after

being misunderstood by some as 'San Telmus'. Feast April 15. Dim: Chemo.

Tente A diminutive of Clemente.

Teo A diminutive of Mateo, Doroteo and other names containing 'teo'.

Teobaldo Germanic *theud* 'people' + *bald* 'daring, bold'. Dim: Teo. English: Theobald.

Teodomiro Germanic *theud* 'people' + *miru* 'protector'.

Teodorico Germanic *theud* 'people' + *ric* 'king'.

Teodoro, Teodoro Greek *theos* 'God' + *doron* 'gift' = 'gift of God'. The name of 146 saints. Dims: Doro, Teo. Fem: Teodora. English: Theodore.

Teodosio Greek *theos* 'God' + *dosis* 'giving'. Dims: Teo, Tocho. Fem: Teodosia.

Teófanes, Teófano Greek *theos* 'God' + *phanein* 'to appear', a name for the Feast of the Epiphany, celebrated January 6.

Teófilo Greek *theos* 'God' + *philos* 'friend'. Dims: Fico, Filo, Téo, Tofi. Fem: Teófila. English: Theophilus.

Tercio, Terciero Latin *tertius* 'third'. A name for a third son. Fem: Terceira.

Terencio, Terence From Terentius, the name of a Roman clan and also of a game field in the city of Rome. Dims: Tencio, Teres. English: Terrence.

Tereso A name of ancient Greek origin, either from *theros* 'summer' or *thereios* 'wild animal'. Dim: Techo. Fem: Teresa.

Tertulo, Tertulio Latin *tertius* 'third'. Tertulius was the name of an illustrious Roman family. Dim: Tulio.

Teseo Greek *theos* 'god'. In Greek myth Theseus was a monster-slayer who had many exciting adventures.

Teyo A diminutive of Eleuterio.

Tiberio From a Roman name, Tiberius, derived from Italy's Tiber River.

Tiburcio Latin Tiburtius ' inhabitant of Tibur [a resort near Rome]'. Dim: Tibo.

Ticho A diminutive of Patricio.

Ticiano From a Roman name, Titianus 'a relative of Titus' (see Tito, below).

Tilán, Tilano Diminutives of Atilano.

Timoteo Greek *time* 'honor' + *theos* 'God' = 'honor to God'. In the New Testament, the name of a companion of Saint Paul. Feast January 26. Dims: Teo, Tim, Timo. Fem: Timotea. English: Timothy.

Tin A diminutive of Martín and other names ending in '-tín'.

Tino A diminutive of Albertino and of other men's names ending in '-tino'.

Tirso From Greek *thyrsos* 'crowned with vines'; the name of a staff carried by worshippers of the god Dionysus.

Tito From Titus, a Roman first name, derived from Tities, the name of an early Roman tribe. San Tito was a disciple of Saint Paul. Feast January 26. This name is also a diminutive of men's names ending in '-ito'. Fem: Tita. English: Titus.

Tizoc Náhuatl 'penitent'. This name is used in Mexico in honor of the grandson of Aztec leader Moctezuma.

Tobalito A diminutive of Cristóbal.

Tobías 'God is good' in Hebrew. This was the name of several men in the Bible. Dims: Tobi, Tobio. English: Tobias, Toby.

Tocho A diminutive of Teodosio and Héctor.

Tofi A diminutive of Teófilo.

Tomás, Tomaso Aramaic for 'twin'. The name of one of the apostles and of Santo Tomás de Aquino (Saint Thomas Aquinas), the 13th century theologian. Feast January 28. Dims: Tomi, Tomy, Tommy. Basque: Toma, Tomax. Galician: Tomé. Fem: Tomasa. English: Thomas.

Tonio, Toño, Toni Diminutives of Antonio and Antoniano.

Toribio Greek: *thorybios* 'noisy'. Santo Toribio de Mongrovejo (1538-1606), an archbishop of Lima, is protector of the rights of native peoples. Feast March 23.

Toro see Taurio

Tranquilino Latin *tranquillus* 'calm, tranquil'. Dim: Quilino. Fem: Tranquilina.

Tranquilo, Tranquillo Latin *tranquillus* 'calm, tranquil'. Dim: Quilo.

Tránsito Latin *transitus* 'passage'. This name was created by early Christians to signify the passage to heaven. Dim: Tancho. Fem: Transina.

Trinidad Spanish for 'trinity'. A name given to both boys and girls. As a middle name, 'de la Santisima Trinidad'. Feast Sunday after Pentecost. Dim: Trini.

Tristán From Drustan, a Celtic name of ancient Britain borne by the hero of the medieval romance, *Tristan and Isolde*. The meaning of the name is not known. Fem: Tristana.

Tulio From a Roman clan name, Tullius, the meaning of which is unknown. Also a diminutive of Tertulio. Fem: Tulia.

Tuni, Tuño Diminutives of Fortuño.

Tupac The name of a deity in Quechua, language of the Inca Empire of South America.

Tur, Turín Diminutives of Arturo.

Tuto A diminutive of Augusto.

Txomin Basque form of Domingo.

Ubaldo Germanic *hug* 'intelligence, spirit' + *bald* 'bold'. Diminutives: Uva, Baldo.

Ugo, Ugón see Hugo

Ulises Latin name of the Greek hero, Odysseus. According to the poet Homer, the name means 'he who makes himself angry'. Dim: Licho. English: Ulysses.

Ulrico Germanic *wulf* 'wolf' + *ric* 'king'. Fem: Ulrica. English: Ulrich.

Umberto see Humberto

Unai Basque for 'shepherd'.

Urbano Latin *urbanus* 'a city dweller'. There were eight popes by this name.

Uriel Hebrew 'God is light'.

Valdemar, Valdemaro, Waldemar, Waldemaro Germanic *wald* 'ruler, governor' + *mar* 'fame'. Dim: Valde.

Valdo A diminutive of Osvaldo. Also a variant form of Waldo

Valente, Valencio Latin *valens, valentis* 'brave, strong'. Fem: Valencia.

Valentín, Valentino From Valentinus, a Roman clan name derived from Latin *valens, valentis* 'brave, strong'. San Valentín (Saint Valentine) is the patron saint of sweethearts and lovers. Feast February 14. Dims: Tin, Tino, Vale. Catalan: Valentí. Basque: Balendin. Fem: Valentina.

Valeriano From a Roman name, Valerianus 'relative of Valerius'. Fem: Valeriana.

Valero, Valerio From the Roman clan name Valerius, derived from Latin *valerus* 'healthy, strong'. San Valero was a 3rd century bishop of Zaragoza, Spain. Feast January 29. Fem: Valeria.

Vasco Spanish for 'Basque'.

Veche A diminutive of Silvestre.

Velasco From Basque *belasco* 'mountainside'. A popular name in the Middle Ages.

Venancio Latin *venator* 'hunter'. Dim: Nancho.

Venceslao see Wenceslao

Ventura, Venturo Originally these were diminutives of the name Buenaventura, Spanish for 'good fortune'.

Venustiano Latin *venustus* 'charming, graceful'. Dim: Tino.

Veraz Spanish for 'truthful'.

Vero Latin *verus* 'truthful'. Fem: Vera.

Veto A diminutive of Silvestre, Silvestro.

Vicente, Vicencio, Vincente Latin *vincens* 'conquering'. Dims: Chente, Chenche. Catalan: Vicenç. Basque: Bingen, Bixintxo. Fem: Vicenta. English: Vincent.

Victor, Victorio, Victoro Latin *victor* 'victor, winner'. A name used by early Christians to signify victory over sin. Dims: Bito, Vicho, Vico, Vito. Basque: Bitor. Fem: Victoria. English: Victor.

Vidal, Vital Latin *vitalis* 'lively, vital'. Fem: Vida.

Vincente see Vicente

Vino A diminutive of Silvino.

Virgilio A Latin diminutive of *virgis* 'branch'. Virgil, a Roman poet, wrote the *Aeneid,* an epic of the founding of Rome. Dims: Gilo, Guilo, Lilo, Quilo.

Virginio Latin *virgo, virginis* 'a virgin'. Dim: Quino. Fem: Virginia.

Vito Latin *vitus* 'alive, vital'. Also a diminutive of Victor. Fem: Vita.

Viviano, Bibiano From Latin *vivus* 'alive'. Dims: Bibi, Nano. Fem: Viviana, Bibiana.

Vladimiro, Bladimiro Slavic *vladi* 'master' + *mir* 'world'. San Vladimiro was the first Russian ruler to convert to Christianity. Feast July 15.

Vulpiano Latin *vulpes* 'fox'.

Waldemaro see Valdemaro

Waldo Germanic *wald* 'governor, ruler'. Also a diminutive of Oswaldo.

Walterio see Gualterio

Wenceslao, Venceslao Czech *vienetz* 'crown' + *slava* 'glory'. This saint of Bohemia, who died in 929, was admired throughout Europe and is remembered in the Christmas carol, 'Good King Wenceslas'. Feast September 28. Fem: Wenceslada. English: Wenceslas.

Wilfredo Germanic *wil* 'will' + *fridu* 'peace'. English: Wilfred.

Xacinto Galician form of Jacinto.

Xacobo Galician form of Jacob.

Xaime Galician form of Jaime.

Xalba Basque form of Salvador.

Xanti Basque form of Santiago.

Xaquím Galician form of Joaquín.

Xarles Basque form of Carlos.

Xavier, Xabier, Javier Basque *etxe berri* 'new house'. Saint Francis Xavier was a founder of the Jesuit order. Feast December 3. Dims: Jave, Javi, Xabi, Xave, Xavi. Catalan: Xaviè. Fem: Xabiera, Xaviera, Javiera.

Ximun Basque form of Simón.

Xoán Galician form of Juan.

Xosé Galician form of José.

Xulio Galician form of Julio.

Xurxo Galician form of Jorge.

Yaco A diminutive of Ciríaco.

Yago see Iago

Yokim Basque form of Joaquín.

Yon Basque form of Juan.

Yoseba Basque form of José.

Ysidro see Isidro

Ysmael see Ismael

Yuli Basque form of Julio.

Zacarías Hebrew 'God has remembered'. The name of more than 30 men in the Bible, including the father of John the Baptist. English: Zachary.

Zeferino see Ceferino

Zenobio, Cenobio Greek *xenos* 'foreigner' + *bios* 'to live'. A name for a monk living apart from society. Dim: Séon. Fem: Zenobia.

Zenón Greek *xenos* 'foreigner'. San Zenón is protector of infants. Feast April 12. Fem: Zenona.

Zoilo Greek *zoe* 'life'. San Zoilo was a 4th century martyr saint of Córdoba, Spain. Feast June 27.

Zósimo Greek *zosimos* 'vigorous'.

Girls' names

Abelina see **Avelina**

Abigaíl 'Joy of her father' in Hebrew. Diminutives: Abi, Abbi, Abby, Gail, Gaila. English: Abigail.

Abila, Abilia Latin *habilis* 'skilled. Masc: Abilo, Abilio.

Abra Feminine form of Abraham.

Abril, Abrila, Abrilia Latin *Aprilis*, the second month of the old Roman calendar. English: April.

Acacia Greek *akakia* 'good'. The name of a flowering tree that symbolizes resurrection. Dim: Cacia. Masc: Acacio.

Ada 'Beauty, ornament' in Hebrew. In the Bible, Adah was the wife of Lamec, mother of Jabel and Jubal. Dims: Adi, Adia, Dina. Also a diminutive of Adela and other names that begin with Ada-.

Adabela, Adabella A blend of Ada and Bela or Bella. Dim: Bela.

Adalía A blend of Ada and Lía.

Adalia The name of the Persian goddess of fire, and also of a woman in the Bible. Dim: Lina.

Adalina This name may be a variant of Adelina (below), or a blend of Ada and a name ending in '-ina', such as Catalina. Dim: Dalina.

Adalsinda Germanic *adal* 'noble' + *sind* 'path'.

Adaluz A blend of Ada and Luz. Dims: Adalucy, Lucita, Lucy, Luz.

Adamaría, Adamari Blends of Ada and María.

Adana Feminine form of Adán (Adam).

Adaniela see Daniela

Adela, Adelia, Edel, Edelia Germanic *adal* 'noble'. Originally diminutives of Adelaida, Adelgunda and other 'Adel-' names. Dims: Ada, Adi, Dela, Lala, Lela, Lita. Masc: Edilio. English: Adele, Ethel.

Adelaida Germanic *adal* 'noble' + *heid* 'kind, sort'. Santa Adelaida (931-999), the wife of the Holy Roman Emperor Otto the Great, is the patron saint of princesses and stepparents. Feast December 16. Dims: Adela, Adelia, Adelita, Alaide, Dalida, Lala, Laya, Lela, Layda. English: Adelaide.

Adelfa Greek *adelpha* 'sister'. Dim: Elfa. Masc: Adelfo.

Adelgunda, Aldegunda Germanic *adal* 'noble' + *gundi* 'war'. Masc: Adelgundis, Aldegundis.

Adelicia A blended name, from Adela and Alicia. Dim: Delicia.

Adelina Spanish version of the French name Adeline. Dims: Alena, Alina, Delina, Deli, Lina. English: Adeline.

Adelinda Germanic *adal* 'noble' + *lind* 'sweet, pleasing'.

Adelma, Edelma Germanic *adal* 'noble' + *helm* 'protector'. Dim: Delma. Masc: Adelmo.

Adi, Adia Diminutives of Ada.

Adiana A blend of Ada and Ana.

Adolfina Fem. of Adolfo, from Germanic *adal* 'noble' + *wulf* 'wolf'. Dim: Fina.

Adonais, Adonia Greek *Adonaia* 'relative of Adonis'. This name was used in ancient Greece as an epithet of Aphrodite, goddess of beauty. Dim: Adona.

Adoración Spanish for 'adoration, worship'. A name bestowed in honor of la Adoración de los Reyes (the Feast of the Epiphany), celebrated January 6. Dim: Dora.

Adriana, Adrianna Latin Hadrianus 'a native of Hadria [a city in Italy on the Adriatic Sea]'. The name of the city comes from a word in the Illyrian language, *adur* 'water'. Dims: Adri, Adria. Masc: Adriano, Adrián. English: Adriana, Adrianna, Adrienne.

Afra Latin *Africa* 'Africa', from Arabic *afar* 'dust'. The 4th century saint, Santa Afra, is venerated at a shrine in Girona, Spain. Feast August 5.

África Latin *Africa* 'Africa', derived from Arabic *afar* 'dust', a reference to the deserts of Northern Africa. A name given in honor of Our Lady of Africa, whose shrine was discovered in Algiers. Feast August 5.

Afrodita, Afrodite From Aphrodite, the Greek goddess of love.

Agapita Feminine of Agapito, an early Christian name from Greek *agape* 'love'. Dim: Ágape, Pita.

Ágata see Águeda

Agi A diminutive of Augustina.

Agnese see Inés

Agostina see Augustina

Agraciana see Graciana

Agripina From a Roman clan name, Agrippinus 'a relative of Agrippa', derived from Latin *agrippa* 'born feet-first'. One of the most prominent Roman family names. Dim: Pina. Masc: Agripino.

Águeda, Ágata Greek *agathos* 'good'. The 3rd century Santa Ágata is patron saint of nurses. Her protection is sought against earthquakes and volcanic eruptions. Feast February 5. English: Agatha.

Agurtzane, Agurne Basque equivalents of Rosario.

Agustina see **Augustina**

Aída, Aida, Ayda Aida is a traditional diminutive form of Adelaida. The name was made especially popular by the 19th century opera *Aida* by Guiseppe Verdi. Dim: Ducha.

Aidée, Aidé see **Haydée**

Ailen, Aillén, Aylen, Ayelén 'Very clear, transparent' in the Araucanian language of Chile and Argentina.

Aina, Ainona Catalan forms of Ana.

Ainoa, Ainhoa A Marian name, from a sanctuary of the Virgin in the Basque region of France. Feast August 15.

Aintzane Basque form of Gloria.

Aixa Arabic 'woman'. The name of the second wife of the prophet Muhammad. English: Aisha.

Alaide A diminutive of Adelaida.

Alameda see **Almeida**

Alana Feminine form of Alán and Alano, which may derive from the name of a nomadic tribe, the Alans, originally from Asia Minor, who were driven into Spain by the Huns in the 4th century. Another possible source is the Celtic word *ail*, which means 'noble'.

Alandra A blend of Alana or Alicia or another 'Al-' name with Sandra. Dim: Landra.

Alansa, Alanza see Alonsa

Alazne Basque equivalent of Milagros.

Alba Latin for 'dawn'. A name bestowed in honor of the Virgin as Nuestra Señora del Alba (Our Lady of the Dawn). This name is popular in the Catalan region of Spain. Feast August 15.

Albana From the Roman name Albana, Latin for a native of any one of several cities in Italy called Alba. The source is Latin *alba* 'white'. Masc: Albán, Albano.

Alberta Germanic *adal* 'noble' + *berht* 'shining, brilliant'. Dims: Berta, Bertita. Masc: Alberto. English: Alberta.

Albertina From the French Albertine, a feminine form of Albert. Dims: Tina, Titina. Masc: Albertino.

Albina From a Roman family name, Albinus, derived from Latin *albus* 'white'. Dim: Albi. Masc: Albino.

Alcira, Alzira, Elcira The name of a city in eastern Spain, from an Arabic word meaning 'island'. Dims: Alci, Cira.

Alda From either Germanic *adal* 'noble' or *ald* 'old, venerable'. A name made popular by medieval romances of chivalry in which Alda was the wife of the hero, Orlando. Masc: Aldo.

Aldana A blend of Alda and Ana.

Aldara A feminine form of Aldemaro.

Aldegunda see Adelgunda

Aldonza This name was invented by the Spanish writer, Miguel de Cervantes. Masc: Aldonso, Aldonzo.

Alegra Spanish *alegre* 'happy, joyful'. Masc: Alegre. English: Allegra.

Alegría Spanish for 'joy'.

Aleida, Aleyda Greek *Altea*, an epithet of Athena, the Greek warrior goddess + *eydos* 'similar to' = 'like Athena'.

Aleixandra Catalan form of Alejandra. Dim: Alexa.

Alejandra, Alesandra, Alessandra From Greek *alexein* 'to defend' + *andros* 'man'. Dims: Alexa, Ali, Lexi, Sandra, Sandi, Sandy, Zandra, Zondra. Catalan: Aleixandra, Alisandra. Basque: Alesandere. Masc: Alejandro. English: Alexandra.

Alejandrina, Alesandrina, Alexandrina Greek *alexein* 'to defend' + *andros* 'man'. Dims: Alexina, Drina, Sandrina. Masc: Alejandrino, Alesandrino, Alexandrino.

Alena, Alina Diminutives of Adelina.

Alesia see Alicia

Aletea, Alitea, Altea Greek *aletheia* 'truth'. María Aletea was a 17th century Spanish princess.

Alexia, Alexa, Aleixa Greek *alexius* 'defender'. Masc: Alejo.

Alexina A diminutive of Alejandrina.

Aleyda see Aleida

Alfa, Alfia From *Alpha*, the first letter of the Greek alphabet. This early Christian name is based on the concept of God as the Alpha and the Omega, the beginning and the end. Masc: Alfeo, Alfio.

Alfi, Alfita Diminutives of Alfreda.

Alfonsa Germanic *al* 'all, totally' + *funs* 'prepared'. Masc: Alfonso, Alfonsino.

Alfonsina Germanic *al* 'all, totally' + *funs* 'prepared', with a Latin name ending.

Alfreda Germanic *alf* 'elf, supernatural being' + *rad* 'advice, counsel'. Dims: Alfi, Alfie, Alfita, Freda, Frida. Masc: Alfredo.

Ali A diminutive of Alejandra, Alejandrina, and of other names beginning with 'Al-'.

Aliana Catalan form of Juliana.

Aliberta see Alberta

Alicia, Alisa, Alita From Aliz, the name of the heroines of several medieval French romances. Alicia is also used as a feminine form of Alejo. Alyssa is a popular variant among North American parents. Dims: Alis, Chita, Licha, Lilí. English: Alice.

Alida, Alidia see Hélida

Alina see Adelina

Alis A diminutive of Alicia.

Alisa A variant of Alicia or Elisa.

Alisandra Catalan form of Alejandra.

Alma Spanish for 'soul, spirit'.

Almaquina The feminine form of Almaquio, from Greek *allos* 'foreign' + *machos* 'combat'. Dims: Alma, Quina.

Almeida, Almeda, Alameda Variants of the name of a a 6th century Welsh saint and princess, Saint Almheda in English. Feast August 1.

Almendra From Spanish *almendro*, 'almond tree'.

Almira Germanic *adal* 'noble' + *mar* 'fame'. Dim: Almi. Masc: Alomar.

Almudena, Almudina Arabic for 'city'. Nuestra Señora de Almudena is the oldest church in Madrid. Feast November 9. Dims: Almunda, Almuda, Almudí, Almudín.

Alodia see Elodia

Aloisa, Aloisia From the Provençal name Aloys, which has the same source as Luis: *hlod* 'glorious' + *wig* 'combat'. Dim: Aloya. Masc: Aloisio.

Alona A recent name, perhaps a variant of Alonsa or Alana. Also the name of a mountain in the Basque region, site of an apparition of Our Lady of Arantzazu.

Alondra A blend of Alana and Sondra.

Alonsa, Alansa, Alanza Germanic *al* 'all' + *funs* 'prepared'. Masc: Alonso.

Aloya A diminutive of Aloisa.

Altagracia Spanish *alta* 'high' + *gracia* 'grace'. A name given in honor of the Virgin Mary as Nuestra Señora de la Altagracia (Our Lady of Highest Grace), patroness of the Dominican Republic. Feast January 21. Dims: Alta, Altina, Tata.

Altea see Aletea

Álvara, Alvera Germanic *adal* 'noble' + *ward* 'guardian'. Masc: Álvaro.

Alvina From either Germanic *alf* 'elf, supernatural being' or *adal* 'noble' + *win* 'friend'. Dims: Alvi, Alvita, Vina. Masc: Alvino.

Alvisa see Elvisa

Alzira see Alcira

Ama A diminutive of names that begin with 'Ama-', including Amapola, Amata and Amadea.

Amada see Amata

Amadea A name created by early Christians from Latin *amare* 'to love' + *Deum* 'God'. Dim: Ama. Masc: Amadeo.

Amadisa Old French Amadis, from Latin *amare* 'to love'. Amadís de Gaula was the hero of a medieval Spanish romance of chivalry. Masc: Amadís.

Amaia, Amaira see Amaya

Amalia Germanic *amal* 'work'. Dims: Lía, Lila, Lita, Maya. See also Amelia.

Amalur, Amalure Basque 'Mother Earth'.

Amancai In the Quechua language, the name of a yellow and red flower.

Amancia Latin *amans* 'loving'. Dim: Mancha. Masc: Amancio.

Amanda Latin *amanda* 'lovable'. Dims: Manda, Mandy. Masc: Amando. English: Amanda.

Amapola Arabic 'poppy'. Dims: Ama, Pola.

Amara A diminutive of Amaranta and Amarilis.

Amaranta Greek *amaranto* 'undying, imperishable'. Dims: Amara, Amarita. Masc: Amaranto.

Amarilis Latin *amaryllis*, from Greek *amarysso* 'to shine'. A favorite name for heroines among Roman writers of the Golden Age. Modern variants include Amaris, Amarissa. Dim: Amara.

Amata, Amada Latin *amata* 'beloved'. Dim: Ama. Masc: Amado.

Amatista Spanish for 'amethyst'.

Amaya, Amaia, Amaira Basque 'a high place'. The name of the heroine of traditional Basque tales of the valiant knight, Teodosio de Goñi.

Ambrosia Greek *ambrosios* 'immortal'. Dim: Bocha. Masc: Ambrosio.

Amelia From a Roman clan name, Aemilius, derived from Latin *aemulus* 'rival'. Dims: Mela, Meli, Melita, Meya. Masc: Amelio. English: Amelia

América From Amerigo, an Italian cognate of the Spanish name Enrique. Both derive from the Germanic *haim* 'home' + *ric* 'king'. Dim: Meca. Masc: Américo.

Aminda, Aminta Greek *amynos* 'defender'. Masc: Amintor.

Amira Feminine of Amir, from Arabic *emir* 'prince'. Dim: Amiri.

Amor, Amora Spanish *amor* 'love'.

Amparo Spanish for 'protection'. This name is given in honor of the Virgin Mary in her role as protectress. Nuestra Señora de los Desamparados, patron of Valencia, Spain, is remembered on the second Sunday in May.

Ana, Anna, Ania 'God has favored me' in Hebrew. According to popular tradition Santa Ana (Saint Anne) was the mother of the Virgin Mary. Though not mentioned in the Bible, she is one of the most widely revered saints in Europe. Feast July 26. Dims: Aneta, Anita, Nana. Catalan: Aina, Ainona. Basque: Ane. English: Ann, Anne, Anna, Hannah.

Anabel, Anabela This is usually considered a Scottish name, though it could just as easily have originated in Spain as a combination of Ana and Isabel.

Anacaona The name of a legendary princess of the Taino people of the Carribean island of Santo Domingo.

Anacleta Greek *anaklesis* 'seeking help'. Masc: Anacleto.

Anahí In the Guarani language 'flower of the ceiba (silk-cotton tree)'. This is the national flower of Argentina and Uruguay.

Anaïs A French variant of Ana made popular by the 20th century writer, Anais Nin. Sometimes used as a variant of Anahí.

Analena A blend of Ana and Elena.

Analía A blend of Ana and Lía.

Analilia A blend of Ana and Lilia.

Analisa A blend of Ana and Elisa. Variant spellings include Analissa, Analise, Anelisa, Annelisa, Annelise.

Analola A blend of Ana and Lola.

Anamaría, Annamaría Blends of Ana or Anna and María.

Anarosa A blend of Ana and Rosa.

Anastasia Greek *anastasis* 'resurrection'. In European popular tradition, this was the name of the Virgin Mary's midwife (she is not mentioned in the Bible). Feast December 25. Dims: Tacha, Tacia, Tasha. Masc: Anastasio. English: Anastasia.

Anatilde A blend of Ana and Matilde.

Anatolia Greek *anatole* 'dawn, the east'. Dim: Tolia. Masc: Anatolio.

Andeana Spanish 'woman of the Andes'.

Andone Basque form of Antonia.

Andrea, Andresa, Andera, Andria Feminine forms of Andrés, from the Greek *andros* 'man'. Basque: Andere. English: Andrea.

Andreana A blend of Andrea and Ana.

Andreína A blend of Andrea and Reina.

Andrica A blend of Andrea and a name ending in '-ica', such as Federica.

Ane Basque form of Ana.

Anélida A blend of Ana and Élida.

Añes Basque form of Inés.

Aneta A diminutive of Ana by way of a French variant, Annette.

Ángela Greek *angelos,* which meant 'messenger' in classical times and 'angel' in Christian times. Santa Ángela Merici established the Ursuline Order of nuns in the 16th century. Feast January 27. Dims: Ange, Angelina. Masc: Ángel, Angelo. English: Angela.

Ángeles 'Angels' in Spanish, from the Marian name Nuestra Señora de los Ángeles (Our Lady of the Angels), patroness of Costa Rica and L.A. Feast August 2. As a second name, 'de los Ángeles'. Dims: Ange, Angelina, Angelines.

Angélica Latin *angelica* 'like an angel'. The name of the heroine of the epic romance, *Orlando Furioso,* by the Italian writer Ludovigo Ariosto (1474-1533). English: Angelica

Angelina From a French diminutive of Ángela. Dim: Lina. English: Angelina.

Angelines A diminutive of Ángeles.

Angustias, Angustia Latin *angustias* 'difficulties', a name for the Virgin Mary as Nuestra Señora de las Angustias, the patroness of Granada, Spain. Feast September 15.

Ania see Ana

Aniana Latin *agnus* 'lamb'. Masculine: Aniano.

Aniceta Greek *aniketos* 'invincible'. Dims: Anica, Cheta. Masc: Aniceto.

Anisia, Anisa, Anissa Latin *anisum* 'the anise plant'.

Anita, Anitia These names originated as diminutives of Ana. Dim: Nita.

Annabel see Anabel

Annora, Anora see Honor

Anselma Germanic *Ans,* a god name + *helm* 'protector'. Dims: Selma, Chelma. Masc: Anselmo.

Antéa, Antía Greek *antheia* 'flowery', an epithet of the goddess Hera, wife of Zeus. Sometimes used as a diminutive of Antonia or as a feminine form of Antéo.

Antolia, Antolina, Antoliana Feminine forms of Antolín (a variant of Antonio). Dims: Lina, Lana.

Antonia From Antonius, a Roman name of Etruscan origin, the meaning of which is not known. Dims: Tonia, Toña. Masc: Antonio. English: Antonia.

Antonieta, Antoneta Spanish forms of Antoinette, a French cognate of Antonia.

Antonina From the Latin name Antonina 'a relative of Antonius'. Dim: Nina. Masc: Antonino.

Anunciación, Anunciata, Latin *adnuntio* 'announce', signifying the announcement made to Mary that she would bear the Christ Child. Feast March 25. Dims: Anuncia, Nuncia, Chon, Chona.

Aparición Spanish for 'apparition', the appearance of Christ to the apostles after the resurrection.

Apolinaria Latin *apollinarus* 'sacred to Apollo', Roman god of archery, poetry, prophecy and the sun. Dims: Loni, Pola. Masc: Apolinario.

Apolonia Latin Apollo, the Roman god of archery, poetry, prophecy and the sun. Santa Apolonia was a 3rd century martyr.

Feast February 9. Dims: Loña, Loni, Pola. Masc: Apolonio. English: Apollonia.

Aquilina From a Roman family name, Aquilinus, derived from Latin *aquilo* 'north wind'. Dims: Aquita, Aquilita, Lina. Masc: Aquilino.

Ara A diminutive of Arabela and Araceli.

Arabela Latin *ara* 'altar' + *bela* 'beautiful'. This name was first used in Scotland in the 13th century,. Dims: Ara, Bela.

Araceli, Aracely, Arcelia, Aricela Latin *ara* 'altar' + *caeli* 'of heaven'. The shrine of Ara Coeli in Rome marks the site of an apparition of the Virgin to the Emperor Constantine. There is also a shrine by this name in Córdoba, Spain. Feast May 2. Dim: Ara, Celia, Chela, Cheli.

Arantxa, Arancha, Aranzazu, Arantzazu Basque 'thorn bush' or 'voice in the thorn bush'. A shrine by this name commemorates an apparition of the Virgin Mary in Oñate in 1469. Feast August 15.

Arcadia Greek Arkadios, a name for a native of the Greek province of Arcadia, legendary home of Arcas, son of Zeus. Dims: Cadia. Masc: Arcadio.

Arcángela Spanish for 'archangel'. Masc: Arcángel.

Argenta, Argentina Spanish *argento* 'silver'. Dim: Tina.

Aria A diminutive of Ariadna, Ariana.

Ariadna, Ariana Greek *ariadnos* 'most holy'. In myth, Ariadna was the beloved of the hero Theseus. Dim: Aria. English: Ariana.

Ariela, Arela Feminine forms of Ariel, from a Hebrew name which may mean either 'hero' or 'hearth'. Masc: Ariel, Arel, Arielo. English: Ariel, Arielle.

Aristea From Aristaeus, the name of the Greek god of beekeeping, protector of fruit trees. Dim: Tea. Masc: Aristeo.

Armanda, Arminda Germanic *hard* 'strong, brave' + *man* 'man'. Dims: Minda, Mandy. Masc: Armando.

Armida A name of unknown origin that was popularized in the Renaissance by Italian poet Torquato Tasso.

Armonia see Harmodia

Arnolda, Arnalda Germanic *arn* 'eagle' + *wald* 'ruler'. Diminutive: Nola. Masc: Arnoldo, Arnaldo.

Arona Feminine form of Arón.

Arroin Basque form of Pilar.

Arsenia Greek *arsen* 'energetic'. Masc: Arsenio.

Artemisa, Artemisia Artemis was the Greek goddess of the moon, of hunting and childbirth, and patroness of unmarried young women. Dim: Micha. Masc: Artemio. English: Artemis, Artemisia.

Ascensión Spanish for 'ascent'. A name honoring the Virgin Mary, referring to her ascension to heaven. Feast August 15. Dims: Ascensi, Chencho, Chon.

Asela The name of a 4th century saint. The meaning and origin of the name are not known.

Aspasia Greek *aspasia* 'welcome'. Masc: Aspasio.

Asteria, Astra, Astrea Greek *aster* 'star'. In Greek myth, Asteria was pursued by Zeus and transformed into the island of Delos, the birthplace of Apollo and Artemis. Masc: Asterio.

Astrid From Old Norse *As,* a goddess name + *frithr* 'beautiful'.

Asunción Spanish 'assumption'. A name bestowed in honor of la Asunción de la Virgen (the Virgin Mary's ascension to heaven). María Asunción is patroness of Paraguay. Feast August 15. Dims: Chon, Asunta. See also Ascensión.

Atala, Atalaya Greek *attalos* 'young'.

Atanasia Greek *athanasia* 'immortal'. Dim: Nacha. Masc: Atanasio.

Atenea, Athena A Greek warrior goddess, patroness of Athens. Dim: Thena. English: Athena.

Atocha Arabic 'feather grass'. A shrine in Madrid is dedicated to the Virgin as Nuestra Señora de Atocha. Dim: Taucha.

Atsegiñe Basque form of Consuelo.

Atzimba 'Relative of the king' in the native Tarascan language of Mexico. The name of a 16th century princess.

Augusta Latin *augustus* 'old, venerable'. Augustus was the name of one of Rome's most distinguished families. Masc: Augusto. English: Augusta.

Augustina, Agustina, Agostina From a Roman clan name, Augustinus 'a relative of Augustus', derived from Latin *augustus* 'old, venerable'. Augustus was a title given to Roman emperors. Dims: Agi, Tina. Masc: Augustino, Agustino.

Aura Latin *aura* 'breath wind'.

Áurea, Áuria, Oria Latin *aurea* 'golden'. Masc: Áureo.

Aurelia, Oralia, Orelia From the Roman clan name Aurelius, derived from Latin *aurea* 'golden'. Dims: Aura, Ora. Masc: Aurelio.

Aureliana From Aurelianus 'a relative of Aurelius' in Latin. Masc: Aureliano.

Auristela Latin *aurea* 'golden' + *stella* 'star', an allusion to the Virgin Mary.

Aurora, Orora Aurora was the Roman goddess of dawn. Dims: Aurita, Ora.

Austreberta Germanic *austro* 'east' + *berht* 'famous, shining'. Masc: Austreberto.

Avelina, Aveliana, Abelina From a medieval French name, Aveline, a diminutive of Latin *avis* 'bird'. Dim: Lina. Masc: Avelino. English: Aveline.

Avril, Avrila, Avrilia see Abril

Aylen, Ayelen see Ailen

Ayuda Spanish for 'assistance, help'. A name given in honor of the Virgin as Nuestra Señora de Ayuda Perpetua (Our Lady of Perpetual Help). Feast February 2.

Azucena From an Arabic word for 'lily', symbol of the Virgin Mary.

Bab, Babita Diminutives of Bárbara.

Babet A diminutive of Elisabet.

Baia A diminutive of Eulalia.

Balbina Latin *balbus* 'stammering'. Dim: Bina. Masc: Balbino.

Baldomera Germanic *bald* 'daring, bold' + *miru* 'protector'. Masc: Baldomero.

Bárbara Latin *barbara* 'foreigner'. Santa Bárbara, who lived in Syria in the 3rd century, is the patron saint of architects, masons, engineers and makers of fireworks. Her feast is celebrated December 5. Dims: Bab, Babita, Barbi, Barbrita, Basha, Bobbi. Masc: Barbarito. English: Barbara.

Bartolomea A feminine form of Bartolomé (English Bartholomew) from the Aramaic *bar* 'son of' + Tolmaï, a personal name. The 19th century Italian saint Bartolomea Capitaneo established a free school for poor children. Feast July 27. Dim: Bartita, Bartola, Tola.

Basha A diminutive of Bárbara.

Basilia, Basilea Greek *basileus* 'king'. Masc: Basilio, Basileo, Basilo.

Beatriz, Beatrix, Beatrisa Latin *beata* 'saintly, blessed'. Dims: Bea, Beata, Bebe, Beta, Beti, Bita, Ticha, Trixi, Trixy. Catalan: Beatriu. Basque: Batirtze. Galician: Beta. English: Beatrice.

Becha A diminutive of Betsabé.

Begoñe, Begoña Basque 'place of the high hill', site of the shrine of Nuestra Señora de Begoñe, patroness of Vizcaya. Feast October 11.

Begonia A flower name. Also an alternative spelling of Begoñe.

Bel, Belita Diminutives of Belén and of names ending in '-bel' and '-bela'.

Bela, Bella From the Late Latin and Italian name Bella, meaning 'beautiful'. Also a diminutive of names containing 'bel' and 'bela'.

Belarmina From the family name of the Italian saint, Roberto Belarmino. The derivation of the name is uncertain. Feast May 13. Masc: Belarmino.

Belén Spanish for Bethlehem, birthplace of Jesus, from Hebrew 'house of bread', a reference to the fertile fields near the town. This name is bestowed in honor of the Virgin Mary as Nuestra Señora de Belén (Our Lady of Bethlehem). Feast December 25. Dims: Bel, Belita. Basque: Ostatxu.

Belicia see Isabel

Belina A diminutive of Bela, Isabel and other 'bel' names.

Belinda From the old Germanic name, Betlindis. Its meaning is unknown, except that it contains the name-element *lind* 'pleasing'. In medieval romances, Belinda was the name of the wife of the knight Orlando. Dims: Bel, Bela, Linda.

Belisa A Latin name made popular by the poems of Spanish poet Lope de Vega. Dim: Lisa.

Belisaria Latin *belis* 'pledge'. Belisarius was the name of a 6th century Byzantine general. Masc: Belisario.

Belita A diminutive of Belén and other names containing 'bel'.

Benigna Latin *benigna* 'kind, friendly'. Dim: Nina. Masc: Benigno.

Benita, Benedicta From Latin *benedictus* 'blessed'. Masc. Benito, Benedicto.

Benjamina The feminine form of Benjamín, which means 'son of the right hand' in Hebrew. Dim: Mina.

Bequi A diminutive of Rebeca.

Berenguela Germanic *bern* 'a bear' + *gar* 'a spear'. Masc: Berenguer.

Berenice, Bernicia Greek *pherein* 'to bring' + *nike* 'victory'. The name of a 4th century Syrian saint. Feast October 4. Dims: Bere, Bernita. English: Bernice.

Bernabela A feminine form of Bernabé, from Hebrew 'son of encouragement'.

Bernadeta, Bernadetta Spanish form of the French name Bernadette, from Germanic *bern* 'a bear'. Santa Bernadeta witnessed the apparition of the Virgin Mary at Lourdes, France, in 1858. Feast February 18. English: Bernadette.

Bernarda Germanic: *bern* 'a bear' + *hard* 'strong, brave'. Masc: Bernard.

Bernardina Germanic *bern* 'a bear' + *hard* 'strong, brave', with a Latin name ending. Dim: Dina. Masc: Bernardino. English: Bernardine.

Bernice, Bernicia see Berenice

Bernita A diminutive of Berenice.

Berta Germanic *berht* 'shining, brilliant'. Berthe, or Perchta, was the name of an old Germanic Earth goddess who was once considered an ancestress by kings and queens of Europe. Dims: Bertalina, Beta, Beti. Masculine: Berto. English: Bertha.

Bertibla, Bertila, Bertilia, Bertilla Variants of the Latin name Bertibilis, derived from the Germanic *berht* 'shining, brilliant'. Masc: Bertilo, Bertilio.

Beta see Berta

Beta, Beti Diminutives of Beatriz.

Beti, Betsi Diminutives of Elisabet.

Betsabé An Old Testament name which could mean 'the opulent one' or 'seventh daughter'. Dims: Becha, Betsi. English: Bathsheba.

Bianca see Blanca

Bibi A diminutive of Viviana, Bibiana.

Bibiana see Viviana

Bienvenida Spanish for 'welcomed one'. A name for a long-wished-for child. Masc: Bienvenido.

Bina A diminutive of Balbina.

Bique A diminutive of Victoria.

Bita A diminutive of Beatriz, Victoria.

Blanca, Bianca From the Old French *blanc* 'white', signifying purity of heart. This was the name of a 12th century queen of Navarre. The Italian cognate,

Bianca, is also popular. Feast August 5. Dims: Blancha, Blanchi, Blanquita, Quita. Basque: Zuri. Masc: Blanco. English: Blanche.

Blanda Latin *blandus* 'flattering'. Dims: Blandina, Dina. Masc: Blandino.

Blasa Latin *blaesus* 'lisping, stuttering'. Masc: Blas.

Bona Latin *bona* 'good'. Bona Dea was a Roman goddess of chastity and fertility. A celebration was held in her honor each May 1.

Bonfilia From Latin *bona* 'good' + *filia* 'daughter'.

Bonifacia An early Christian name from Latin *boni* 'good works' + *facio* 'to do' = 'to do good works'. Dims: Boni, Facha. Masc: Bonifacio.

Bonita Spanish for 'pretty'. Dims: Boni, Nita.

Borjita From the family name of a 16th century Spanish saint, San Francisco de Borja y Aragón. Masc: Borja.

Braulia Germanic *brand* 'sword'. Masc: Braulio.

Briana, Brianna, Bryana Feminine forms of Brian, an Irish royal name, from Celtic *brig* 'high, noble'.

Bricia From Brictius, the Gaulish (continental Celtic) name of a popular early saint, San Bricio (Saint Brice). Bricia is also a diminutive of Fabricia.

Brígida, Brigidia From Brighíd, a goddess name derived from Celic *brig* 'high, mighty'. The Irish Santa Brígida (Saint Brigid) is the patron saint of scholars. Feast February 1. Another Brígida, who lived in the 14th century, is the patron saint of Sweden and Hungary. Feast July 23. Dims: Bridita, Gidita. English: Brigid, Bridget.

Bruna Germanic *brun* 'brown'. Masc: Bruno.

Brunela Latin diminutive of Germanic *brun* 'brown'.

Buena Spanish for 'good'.

Cacia A diminutive of Acacia.

Cadia A diminutive of Arcadia.

Caela, Caila Diminutives of Micaela.

Caledonia see Celedonia

Calixta, Calista The name of a nymph in Greek myth, from *kallistos* 'the most beautiful'. Dim: Cali. Masc: Calixto, Calisto. English: Callista, Calista.

Camelia In myth, the name of a nymph serving the goddess Diana. Dim: Melia.

Camerina Latin 'a native of Cameria [an ancient Sabine city in Italy]'. Masc: Camerino.

Camila, Camilla In Roman legend, this was the name of a warrior queen. The origin and meaning of the name are not known. Dims: Cama, Mila, Mili. Masc: Camilo. English: Camilla, Camille.

Caña A diminutive of Encarnación.

Cancia, Canciana Latin *cantus* 'song'. Masc: Cancio, Canciano.

Cancianila From a Latin diminutive of *cantus* 'song'.

Candelaria Latin *candela* 'candle'. A Marian name. Nuestra Señora de la Candelaria (after the feast of Candlemas) is patroness of Santa Cruz de Tenerife. Feast February 2. Dims: Canda, Candi, Candela, Candelana, Candelas, Canducha. Masc: Candelario.

Cándida Latin *candida* 'shining, white'. The name of a first century Italian saint who was cured by Saint Paul. Dims: Canda, Candi, Candia. Masc: Cándido.

Caparina 'Butterfly' in Spain's Asturian language.

Cara, Cari Diminutives of Carina, Caridad and Carolina.

Caridad Spanish for 'charity'. A name bestowed in honor of Mary as Nuestra Señora de Caridad (Our Lady of Charity), patroness of Cuba. Feast September 8. Dims: Cara, Cari, Carita.

Carilla See Carla

Carina, Karina, Karena Greek *xarino* 'gracious'. Dims: Cara, Cari, Carín, Karen. Masc: Carino. English: Karen.

Carisa A blended name, probably from a 'Car-' name plus Elisa.

Carla, Carola, Karla Feminine form of Carlos, from the Germanic *karl* 'strong man'. Dims: Carilla, Carlina, Carlita, Carleta. English: Carla.

Carlota A feminine form of Carlos that is popular in Catalunya. Dims: Lola, Loti. English: Carlotta, Charlotte.

Carmel, Carmela Hebrew 'garden'. The convent on Mount Carmel in the Holy Land was dedicated to the Virgin Mary as Our Lady of Mount Carmel. Feast July 16. Dims: Carmelina, Lita, Mela, Melina, Melita. Masc: Carmelo.

Carmelina A diminutive of Carmel. Its diminutive is Mina.

Carmelita Originally a diminutive of Carmel. Dim: Lilí.

Carmen, Carmena, Carmín, Carmina, Carmiña Variants of the name Carmel, from Our Lady of Mount Carmel, influenced by Spanish word for 'song', *carmen*. Carmen was the name of the heroine of a popular 19th century opera by Georges Bizet. Feast July 16. Dims: Carmita, Carmucha, Chita, Mina. Catalan: Carme. Basque: Karmele.

Carola, Carol Variant forms of Carla, influenced by the English name, Carol.

Carolina, Carolena From Caroline, a French diminutive of Carole (cognate of Spanish Carla). Dims: Cara, Cari, Lina, Lolita. English: Caroline, Carolyn.

Carona see Corona

Casandra The daughter of the king of Troy in the Greek epic, the *Iliad*. This name became popular in the Middle Ages along with tales of the Trojan War. Dims: Casey, Kasey, Sande, Sandra, Sandy. English: Cassandra.

Casey Modern diminutive of Casandra, Casia and other 'Cas-' names.

Casia From the Roman clan name Cassius, derived from Latin *cassi* 'metal helmet'. Dims: Casey, Casi, Kasey. Masc: Casio.

Casiana From Cassius, the name of a Roman clan, derived from Latin *cassi* 'metal helmet'. Dim: Chana. Masc: Casiano.

Casilda Arabic 'to sing'. A shrine and a pool near Burgos, Spain, are dedicated to Santa Casilda. Couples who wish to have children toss stones into the pool. Dim: Silde. Masc: Casildo.

Casimira Feminine form of Casimiro, from the Slavic *kasic* 'to destroy' + *meri* 'great'. The name of a 15th century Polish king and saint.

Casta Latin *casta* 'pure'. Masc: Casto.

Castalia Greek *kasteia* 'purity'. In Greek myth, the nymph Castalia was transformed into a fountain. Dim: Talia.

Castana A blend of Casta and Ana.

Castarina A blend of Casta and Catalina.

Cástora Greek *castor* 'beaver'. Feminine form of Cástoro, a name from Greek myth. Castor and Pollux are the twins of the constellation Gemini.

Catalina, Catarina, Catelina, Caterina, Catalín Greek *katharos* 'pure'. Santa Catalina (Saint Catherine) was a 4th century martyr of Alexandria, Egypt. She is patron saint of young girls, spinners and millers. Feast April 29. Another Santa Catalina, of Bologna, Italy, was known for her visions and her miniatures, and is the patron saint of artists. Feast March 9. Dims: Cata, Cate, Cati, Catia, Catina, Catrina, Katerina, Kati, Katina, Katixa, Katrina, Trina. Catalan: Caterina. Basque: Katarin, Katariñe. Masc: Catalino, Catarino. English: Catherine, Katherine.

Cayetana, Gayetana Latin Caietanus 'a native of of Caete [a city in Italy]'. Masc: Cayetano, Gayetano.

Cecilia From the Roman clan name, Caecilius, derived from the Latin *caecus* 'blind'. Santa Cecilia, a popular saint of the Middle Ages, is patroness of poets and musicians. Feast November 22. Dims: Ceci, Cecili, Celia, Chela. Masc: Cecilio. English: Cecilia.

Ceferina, Cefereina Latin *zepherinus* 'west wind'. Dims: Sefia, Rina. Masc: Ceferino.

Cela Diminutive of Celedonia, Celeste.

Celedonia, Caledonia Greek *chelidonon* 'a swallow'. Dims: Cali, Cela, Celi. Masc: Caledonio, Celedonio.

Celerina Latin *celer* 'fast, swift'. Masc: Celerino.

Celeste, Celesta Latin *caelestis* 'heavenly'. Dims: Cela, Cele. English: Celeste.

Celestina Latin *caelestinus* 'celestial'. Dims: Celina, Tina. Masc: Celestino.

Celi A diminutive of Celedonia, Celia and Celina.

Celia From Caelius, a Roman clan name derived from Latin *caelum* 'sky, heaven'. Also a dim. of Araceli and Cecilia. Dims: Celi, Celita. Masc: Celio. English: Celia.

Celina, Celinia From the Roman name Caelinus 'a relative of Caelius', derived from Latin *caelum* 'sky, heaven'. Celina is also used as a diminutive of Celestina. Dim: Lina. Masc: Celino.

Celinda A blend of Celia and Linda.

Celmira see Zelmira

Celsa Latin *celsus* 'lofty, high'. Masc: Celso.

Cenci A diminutive of Inocencia.

Cenita A diminutive of Zenona.

Cenobia see Zenobia

Ceria From Ceres, the Latin name of the Roman goddess of grain, harvest and abundance. Dim: Ceri.

Cesaria, Cesárea From a Roman name, Cesareus 'a relative of Caesar', which may be derived from Latin *caesaries* 'having abundant hair'. Dim: Cesarina. Masc: César, Cesáreo, Cesaro.

Chaba A diminutive of Salvadora.

Chabel, Chabela Diminutives of Isabel and Isabela.

Chala, Chali Diminutives of Rosalía.

Chalina A diminutive of Rosalina.

Chalo A diminutive of Rosario.

Chana A diminutive of names ending in '-iana', such as Casiana and Sebastiana.

Charín, Charo Diminutives of Rosario.

Chava A diminutive of Gustava.

Chayo A diminutive of Rosario.

Cheba A diminutive of Eusebia, Josefa.

Chefa A diminutive of Josefa.

Chela A diminutive of Araceli, Arcelia, Cecilia, Graciela and Marcela

Cheli A diminutive of Araceli.

Chelma A diminutive of Anselma.

Chelo A diminutive of Consuelo.

Chencha A diminutive of Fulgencia and Crescencia

Chenchi A diminutive of Inocencia.

Chencho A diminutive of Ascensión.

Chenda A diminutive of Rosenda.

Chepa A diminutive of Josefa.

Cheta A diminutive of Aniceta.

Cheya A diminutive of Graciela.

Chicha A diminutive of Marcia, Narcisa and Francisca.

China A diminutive of Joaquina.

Chinta A diminutive of Jacinta.

Chita A diminutive of Alicia, Carmen, Felicita, Felícitas, Jesusa and Luz.

Chiva A diminutive of Silvia.

Chloe see Cloe

Chofa A diminutive of Josefa.

Chofi A diminutive of Sofía.

Chola, Chole Diminutives of Isolda and Soledad.

Chon, Chona Diminutives of Concepción. Asunción and other names ending in '-ción'.

Chris- names see Cris-.

Chucha, Chuchita, Chuyita Diminutives of Jesusa.

Cielo Spanish for 'sky'.

Cilla A diminutive of Priscilla.

Cindia, Cintia, Cinzia see Cynthia

Cinta Spanish for 'band, ribbon'. A Marian name, after Nuestra Señora de la Cinta, the patroness of Tortosa, Spain, where she is venerated by pregnant women. Feast first Saturday of September. Also a diminutive of Jacinta.

Cipriana, Ciprina Latin *Cypriana* 'a native of the island of Cyprus', from a Sumerian word for copper, a mineral mined on that island since ancient times. Dim: Chana. Masc: Cipriano.

Cira Greek *kyrios* 'master'. Also a diminutive of Alcira. Masc: Ciro.

Cirenia Cyrene was a nymph in Greek myth who was able to overcome a lion without using weapons. Masc: Cireneo.

Ciríaca Greek *kyrios* 'master'. Masc: Ciríaco.

Cirila Greek *kyrios* 'master'. Dim: Ciri. Masc: Cirilo.

Cisa A diminutive of Narcisa.

Citlali 'Star' in the native Nahuatl language of Central America.

Clara Latin *claro* 'bright, clear'. The 12th century saint, Santa Clara de Asís, gave up a life of luxury to found the order of the Poor Clares. Feast August 11. Dims: Clareta, Clari. Masc: Claro. English: Claire, Clare, Clara.

Claribel A blend of Clara and Isabel. A name popularized by Shakespeare in his play, *The Tempest*.

Clarinda Probably a blend of Clara and Linda. This name became popular in the 16th century, after English poet Edmund Spenser used it in his *Faerie Queene*.

Clarisa The Spanish form of Clarice, a French name made popular by medieval romances of Huon of Bordeaux.

Claudia From Claudius, name of two Roman clans, derived from Latin *claudus* 'limping'. In the Bible, Claudia was a Roman follower of Jesus. Dim: Claudeta. Masc: Claudio. English: Claudia.

Claudina Latin 'a relative of Claudius'. Masc: Claudino. English: Claudine.

Clea A diminutive of Cleopatra.

Clelia, Cloelia Cloelia was a Latin name borne by a legendary Roman heroine who eluded an Etruscan captor by swimming the Tiber River.

Clemencia Latin *clementia* 'mercy'. Dim: Mencha. Masc: Clemente, Clemencio.

Clementina Latin *clemens, clementis* 'merciful'. Dim: Clema. Masc: Clementino. English: Clementine.

Cleofé Greek *kleo* 'celebrate' + *phasis* 'the rising of a star'. Dim: Cleo. Masc: Cleofás.

Cleopatra Greek *kleos* 'glory' + *pater* 'father' = 'glory of her father'. A royal name of ancient Egypt. The best-known Cleopatra ruled Egypt in the 1st century BC. Dims: Cleo, Clea.

Clío Greek *kleio* 'glory'. In Greek myth, Clío was the name of the muse of fame and reputation.

Clodita A diminutive of Clotilde.

Clodomira Germanic *hrod* 'glorious' + *miru* 'protector'. Dims: Clodi, Clodina. Masc: Clodomiro.

Clodovea Germanic *hrod* 'glorious' + *wig* 'warrior'. Masc: Clodoveo.

Cloe, Chloe Greek *khloe* 'green grass', an epithet of the goddess Demeter.

Cloelia see Clelia

Clorinda A blend of the Greek *chlora* 'green' and the Germanic name-element *lind* 'sweet, pleasing'. A name made popular during the Renaissance by Italian poet Torquato Tasso. Dims: Clora, Clori, Clorita.

Clotilde, Clotilda Germanic *hlod* 'glorious' + *hild* 'combat'. The 5th century Santa Clotilda converted her husband, King Clovis of France, to Christianity. She is patron saint of adopted children. Feast June 3. Dims: Clodita, Cloti, Tila, Tilda.

Coco A diminutive of Coleta, Socorro.

Còia Catalan diminutive of Misericordia.

Colasa A diminutive of Nicolasa.

Coleta Spanish form of Colette, a French diminutive of Nicolas. Dim: Coco.

Coloma Catalan form of Paloma.

Columbina Diminutive of Latin *columba* 'a dove'. Also the name of a flower, the columbine.

Concelia A diminutive of Consuelo.

Concepción Spanish for 'conception'. This name refers to La Inmaculada Concepción de María (the Immaculate Conception of Mary). Feast December 8. Dims: Chon, Chona, Concha, Conchi, Concheta, Conchita. Basque: Kontxexi, Sorne, Sorkunde. Catalan: Concepció.

Concha A diminutive of Concepción.

Concheta, Conchetta Diminutives of Concepción from the Italian form of the name, Concetta.

Consejo, Conseja Spanish *consejo* 'advice counsel'. A name honoring Nuestra Señora del Buen Consejo (Our Lady of Good Counsel). Feast April 26.

Consolación Spanish for 'consolation'. A Marian name bestowed in honor of the Virgin Mary as Nuestra Señora de Consolación (Our Lady of Consolation). Feast September 4.

Constancia, Constanta Latin *constantia* 'perseverance, steadfastness'. Diminutives: Stanza, Tancha. Masc: Constancio. English: Constance.

Constantina From the Roman family name Constantinus, derived from Latin *constantia* 'perseverance, steadfastness'. Dim: Tina. Masc: Constantino.

Consuelo, Consuela Consuelo is Spanish for 'consolation, solace'. These names are given in honor of the Virgin Mary as Nuestra Señora del Divino Consuelo (Our Lady of Solace). Dims: Chela, Chelo, Concelia, Suelo, Suela, Suelita. Basque: Atsegiñe.

Cora Greek *kore* 'maiden', epithet of the goddess Persephone. Cora is also a diminutive of Socorro and Corazon. Dims: Coreta, Corina.

Corabel A blend of Cora and Isabel.

Coralia, Coral Late Latin *corallium* 'coral'. Dims: Coralí, Coralina.

Coralinda A blend of Cora and Linda.

Corazón, Corazana Spanish *corazón* 'heart'. A name referring to the Immaculate Heart of Mary. Dims: Cori, Cory.

Cordelia, Cordela This name was made popular by Shakespeare's play, *King Lear*. Cordelia was one of the king's daughters. Shakespeare based this name on Cordula, a Late Latin diminutive of *cor* 'heart'.

Coreta From Corette, a French diminutive of Cora.

Cori A diminutive of Misericordia.

Corina, Corena Spanish form of the French name, Corrine, from Greek *kore* 'maiden'.

Cornelia, Cornalia From a Roman family name, Cornelius, probably derived from Latin *cornelium* 'little horn'. Dims: Cornela, Cornelita, Neli, Nelia, Nélida, Nelly. Masc: Cornelio. English: Cornelia.

Corona Latin *corona* 'crown, garland'. An early Christian name, signifying the crown of martyrdom.

Cósima Greek *kosmas* 'order, beauty'. Masc: Cosme.

Coyo A diminutive of Socorro.

Crescencia Latin *crescens* 'growing'. Dim: Chencha. Masc: Crescencio.

Cris A diminutive of 'Cris-' names.

Crisana, Chrisana Blends of a name beginning with 'Cris-' or 'Chris-'(such as Crista or Cristina) and Ana. Dim: Cris.

Crisantemo Greek *krisós* 'gold' + *anthos* 'flower' = 'chrysanthemum'. Dims: Crisana, Crisanta, Crisann. Masc: Crisanto.

Crispina From a Roman name Crispinus, derived from Latin *crispus* 'curly-haired'. Dims: Cris, Pina. Masc: Crispín, Crispino.

Crista Greek *Khristos* 'Christ'. Also used as a diminutive of Cristina and Cristolbina. Masc: Cristo. English: Christa.

Cristal Spanish for 'crystal'.

Cristi A diminutive of 'Cris-' names.

Cristina, Cristiana Latin Cristianus 'a follower of Christ'. Dims: Cris, Crista, Cristi, Titina. Basque: Kristiñe. Masc: Cristián. English: Christine, Christina.

Cristolbina The feminine form of Cristóbal, from the *Khristos* 'Christ' + *pherein* 'to carry' = 'carrier of Christ'. Dims: Cris, Chris, Crista, Christa, Cristi, Christi.

Cruz Latin *crux, crucis* 'cross', signifying Christ's death on the cross. Cruz can be either a boy's or a girl's name. As a middle name, 'de la Cruz'. Dims: Crusita, Cucha. Catalan: Creu. Basque: Gurutzi, Guruzne.

Cuca A diminutive of Refugia.

Cucha A diminutive of Cruz.

Custodia Latin *custodia* 'guardian'. An early Christian name. Feast of Los Ángeles Custodios October 2. Masc: Custodio.

Cyntia, Cynthia, Cintia, Cindia, Cinzia Greek *Kynthos,* a mountain in Delos, birthplace of Artemis, the goddess of hunting and the moon, and another name for the goddess. Dims: Cinda, Cindi. English: Cynthia, Cindy.

Dacia Latin name of a region on the lower Danube in present-day Rumania. The name is from *daos*, which meant 'wolf' in a dialect of ancient Greek. Dim: Daci. Masc: Dacio.

Dafne, Dafna, Dafnis Greek *daphne* 'laurel tree'. In Greek myth, Daphne was a nymph who was pursued by the god Apollo. He transformed her into a laurel tree. English: Daphne.

Dahlia From a Central American flower named for Swedish botanist Anders Dahl.

Dalia, Dali Diminutives of Dalila.

Dalida A diminutive of Adelaida.

Dalila, Delila Possibly 'loose hair' in Hebrew. In the Old Testament, it was Delilah who betrayed strongman Samson to the Philistines. Dims: Dalia, Lila. English: Delilah.

Dalina A diminutive of Adalia.

Dalinda A blend of Dalia and Linda.

Dalmacia From Dalmatia, Latin name of a region on the Adriatic Sea, derived from Indo-European *dhal* 'young animal'. Dim: Dalma. Masc: Dalmacio.

Dalmira see Delmira

Dámaris, Damara Greek *damaris* 'calf'. In the Bible, Damaris was a woman converted by Saint Paul. Dims: Mari, Mara.

Damiana From the name of the Greek goddess, Damia, also known as Cybele, who was worshipped throughout the Mediterranean area in ancient times. Dims: Dami, Damia, Damita. Masc: Damián, Damiano.

Daniela, Danela, Danila, Adaniela Feminine forms of Daniel, which means 'God is my judge' in Hebrew. Dims: Dana, Dani, Danita.

Daría Persian *darayaraus* 'active'. Dim: Dari. Masc: Darío.

Dariana A blend of Daría and Ana.

Davina, Davinia, Daviana, Davidia, Davita Feminine forms of David, which means 'beloved' in Hebrew.

Débora, Devora Hebrew 'bee'. Deborah was an Old Testament judge and prophet. 'Deborah's Song' is one of the most ancient portions of the Bible. Dims: Deb, Debbie, Debra. English: Deborah, Debra.

Dela A diminutive of Adela.

Delfina, Delfinia From Delphinia, an epithet of the Greek goddess Artemis at her shrine at Delphi, from Greek *delphis* 'dolphin'. Dims: Delfi, Fina. Masc: Delfín, Delfino. English: Delphine.

Deli A diminutive of Adelina.

Delia An epithet of Diana, the Roman goddess of the moon and of hunting, referring to her birthplace, the island of Delos. Also a diminutive of Cordelia.

Delicia A diminutive of Adelicia.

Delila see Dalila

Delina A diminutive of Deolinda and Adelina.

Delma A diminutive of Adelma.

Delmira, Delmar, Dalmira, Edelmira Germanic *adal* 'noble' + *mar* 'fame'. Masc: Adelmaro, Delmaro, Delmiro.

Delores see Dolores

Demetria, Demetra Greek *Demetria* 'a devotee of Demeter', the Greek mother goddess, divinity of agriculture. Masc: Demetrio. English: Demeter.

Denisa From the French name, Denise, cognate of the Spanish name, Dionisia.

Deolinda see Teodolinda

Desideria Latin *desiderium* 'longing'. A name created by early Christians to express their longing for Christ. Desiré, from the French Désirée, is also used. Dims: Desi, Desirita. Masc: Desiderio.

Destina Spanish for 'destiny'.

Devora see Débora

Devota Latin *devota* 'consecrated'. Santa Devota is patron saint of Monaco and Corsica. Feast January 27.

Deyanira, Dejanira Greek *deion* 'destroy' + *aner* 'man'. The name of the wife of the Greek hero, Hercules.

Diana Diana was the Roman goddess of the moon and of hunting. This name became popular during the Renaissance. Its origin is not known. English: Diana, Diane, Dianne.

Diega A feminine form of Diego. In the Middle Ages, the name Sant Yago (the Spanish form of Saint James) was misunderstood by some as 'San Tiago', and this morphed into 'San Diego'.

Digna, Diña Latin *digna* 'worthy, deserving'.

Dina 'Judgment' in Hebrew. The name of the daughter of Jacob and Leah in the Bible, and also a diminutive of Spanish women's names ending in '-dina', such as Bernardina and Geraldina. English: Dina, Dinah.

Dinora Aramaic 'light'. This name was popularized by the 1859 opera, *Dinorah*, by Giacomo Meyerbeer.

Dionisia, Dionisa Feminine forms of Dionisio, from Dionysios, name of the Greek god of wine and festivals. English: Denise.

Dita A diminutive of Edit and Edita.

Divina, Divinia Latin *divina* 'divine'.

Dolores, Delores Spanish for 'sorrows', A name bestowed in honor of the Virgin Mary as La Virgen de los Dolores (a reference to the Seven Sorrows of Mary). Feast September 15. Dims: Dolo, Dolorita, Lola, Lolicia, Lolita, Lora, Lores. Catalan: Dolors. Basque: Nekane. English: Delores.

Doménica, Domínica see Dominga.

Domiciana From Domitius, a Roman clan name derived from Latin *domus* 'home, house'. Dims: Domi, Domica, Chana. Masc: Domiciano.

Dominga, Domenica From a Late Latin name, Dominica, derived from Latin *domina* 'mistress of the house'. Masc: Domingo, Domenico.

Domitila Latin *domitor* 'one who tames'. Dim: Tila. Masc: Domitilo.

Donatila, Donatela A Late Latin diminutive from *donatus* 'given [by God]'. Dims: Dona, Donina. Masc: Donato.

Donosa Latin *donus* 'gift'. Masc: Donoso.

Dora Greek *doron* 'gift'. Also a diminutive of Adoración and of names ending in '-dora'. Dim: Dori. English: Dora.

Doralinda, Dorinda Blends of Dora and Linda.

Doralisa A blend of Dora and Elisa.

Doraluisa A blend of Dora and Luisa.

Dorelia A blend of Dora and Aurelia or Amelia.

Doris Greek *doron* 'gift'. The name of a Greek sea goddess, the mother of the Nereids.

Dorotea, Doroteia Greek *doron* 'gift' + *theos* 'God' = 'a gift of God'. Dims: Dora, Dori, Doro. Masc: Doroteo. English: Dorothy.

Drina A diminutive of Alejandrina.

Drusila, Drusela Feminine diminutive of the Roman family name, Drusus. This was the name of several women of the imperial families of Rome. In the New Testament, a woman named Drusila was converted by Saint Paul.

Ducha A diminutive of Aída.

Dula, Dulia Greek *doulos* 'servant'.

Dulce Spanish for 'sweet'. In the Middle Ages, the name Dulce was a diminutive of Aldonza.

Duva A diminutive of Eduvigis.

Eda A diminutive of Edit, Edita and Edilia.

Edel, Edelia, Edilia Forms of Adela. English: Ethel.

Edelma see Adelma

Edelmira, Delmira, Dalmira Germanic *adal* 'noble' + *mar* 'fame'. Diminutives: Delmi, Mima, Mimi. Masc: Adelmaro, Delmaro, Delmiro.

Eder Basque for 'beautiful'.

Edila, Edilia see Adela

Edit, Edita Anglo-Saxon *ead* 'happy, rich' + *gyth* 'war'. Diminutives: Eda, Edi, Dita. English: Edith.

Edna 'Pleasure, delight' in Hebrew. The name of several women in the Apocrypha.

Eduarda Anglo-Saxon *ead* 'rich, happy' + *weard* 'guard'. Masc: Eduardo.

Edurne, Edur Basque forms of Nieves.

Eduvigis Germanic *hadu* 'strife' + *wig* 'combat'. Dims: Duva, Vijes.

Egidia Greek *aigidios* 'goat, kid'. Masc: Egidio.

Ela A diminutive of Eleonora and other names beginning in 'El-'. English: Ella.

Eladia see Hélida

Elcira see Alcira

Elda The name of place in Spain which is the site of a shrine of the Virgin Mary as Nuestra Señora de la Soledad. Feast December 1. Dim: Eldi.

Eleadora, Eleodora Greek *helios* 'sun' + *doron* 'gift'.

Elena, Helena Greek *helene* 'sunbeam', from *helios* 'sun'. Santa Elena, who lived in the 4th century, was the mother of the Christian Roman Emperor Constantine. She would become famous as a heroine of medieval religious legends. Dims: Ena, Lena, Leni, Nélida, Nena. English: Ellen, Helen, Helena.

Eleonor, Eleanor, Eleanora, Eleonora, Leonor, Leonora From Alienor, an Old French form of Elena. Dims: Ela, Nora. Basque: Elen. English: Eleanor, Elinor.

Elga see Helga

Eliana, Heliana Greek *helios* 'sun'. Masc: Elián, Eliano, Heliano.

Élida, Élidia see Hélida

Eligia Latin *eligius* 'chosen'. Dim: Ligia.

Elisa Originally a diminutive of Elisabet. Dims: Eli, Isa.

Elisabet, Elisabeth, Elizabet, Elizabeth 'God gives' in Hebrew. In the New Testament, Elizabeth was the mother of John the Baptist. Feast November 5. Santa Elisabet of Portugal is the patron saint of peacemakers. Feast July 4. Dims: Babet, Beti, Betsi, Ela, Eli, Elis, Elisa, Elsa, Licha, Lisa, Liseta. English: Elisabeth, Elizabeth.

Elisenda see Melisenda

Elodia, Alodia, Helodia Latin *alodis* 'propriety'. Santa Elodia, a 9th century martyr, is the patron saint of Huesca, Spain, and of runaways. Feast October 22. Dims: Elodina, Lodia.

Eloísa, Heloísa From Heloise, a French cogtnate of Luisa. Dims: Eloína, Licha, Locha, Lochi. English: Eloise.

Elsa Originally a German diminutive of Elisabet. Dim: Elsi. English: Elsa.

Elvia, Helvia Latin for 'yellowish'. Dim: Elvie.

Elvira, Elvera A popular name, though its origin and meaning are not known. Elvira was the name of four queens of Aragón. Dims: Elvi, Elvina, Virucha. English: Elvira.

Elvisa, Alvisa Germanic *haila* 'healthy, strong' + *vid* 'wide, large'.

Ema, Emma Originally a diminutive of names beginning with 'Em-', such as Emanuela. English: Emma.

Emanuela Feminine of Emanuel, from the Hebrew 'God is with us'. Manuela is a modern form. Dim: Ema.

Emelina Spanish version of the French name Emmeline, derived from Germanic *amal* 'rich'. English: Emmeline.

Emeralda see Esmeralda

Emerenciana Latin *emerere* 'earned'. Masc: Emerenciano.

Emérita Latin *emeritus* 'retired person, a veteran'. Masc: Emérito.

Emilia From Aemilius, a Roman clan name, derived from the Latin *aemulus* 'rival'. Dims: Emi, Lila, Mila, Mili, Mimi. English: Emily.

Emiliana From Aemiliana, a Roman name meaning 'a relative of Aemilius', derived from Latin *aemulus* 'rival'. Santa Emiliana, the aunt of Pope Gregory the Great, is patron saint of single women. Feast January 5. Dims: Emilina, Mili. Masc: Emiliano.

Emperatriz Spanish for 'empress', and a traditional royal title in Spain.

Enara Basque for 'a swallow'.

Encarnación Spanish for 'incarnation'. A name referring to the union of the divine and human in Jesus Christ. Feast Christmas Day. Dims: Caña, Chona. Catalan: Encarna.

Engracia Spanish *en* 'in' + *gracia* 'grace', 'one who is in divine grace'. Dim: Gracia.

Enrica Germanic *haim* 'home' + *ric* 'king'. Masc: Enrique. Dims: Enriqueta, Enriquita, Queta, Riqueta. Masc: Enrique. English: Henrietta.

Enza A diminutive of Lorenza.

Epifana, Epifanía Latin *epiphanius* 'epiphany'. This name was created by early Christians in honor of the feast of the Epiphany, celebrated January 6. Masc: Epifanio.

Ercila, Ercilia see Hersilia

Eréndira 'She who smiles'. The name of an Aztec princess.

Erica, Erika Germanic *ehre* 'honor' or *ewa* 'eternal' + *ric* 'king'. Masc: Erico. English: Erica.

Erlinda see Hermelinda

Erma see Irma

Ermelinda see Hermelinda

Ermina, Erminia see Herminia

Ernesta, Ernestina Germanic *ernst* 'vigor, strength'. Dims: Erna, Tina. Masc: Ernesto, Ernestino. English: Ernestine.

Escolástica Latin *schola* 'school'. Santa Escolástica (480-547) was the sister of San Benito. Her aid is invoked in times of drought. Feast February 10. Dims: Colacho, Colaco.

Eskarne Basque form of Mercedes.

Esmeralda Spanish for 'emerald'. Variants are Esmerelda and Emeralda. Dims: Esma, Esme.

Esperanza Spanish for 'hope'. A name given in honor of the Virgin Mary as Nuestra Señora de la Esperanza. Feast December 18, or the Saturday before Christmas week. Dims: Espe, Lancha, Pera, Perita. Basque: Itxaro.

Estanislada Slavic *stan* 'government' + *slav* 'Slav'. Masc: Estanislao.

Estefanía, Estefana, Estefani, Estebeni Greek *stephanos* 'victorious'. Dims: Fana, Fani, Estefa, Stefa. Masc: Esteban. English: Stephanie.

Estela, Estella From Estelle, a French name derived from Latin *stella* 'star', a name given to honor the Virgin Mary as *Stella Maris*, Star of the Sea. Feast May 25. Dims: Esta, Este, Tela, Teli, Telita. Catalan: Estel. Basque: Itziar, Izarne, Izarra. English: Estelle, Stella.

Ester Persian for 'star'. Dims: Estercita, Teche. English: Esther.

Estíbaliz Basque *estibalitz* 'let it be sweet'. A name for the Virgin Mary as the patroness of Álava, Spain. Feast September 12.

Estrella Spanish for 'star'. See Estela.

Etelvina Germanic *adal* 'noble' + *win* 'friend'. Dims: Telina, Vina. Masc: Etelvino.

Eudosia, Eudoxia Greek *eu doxa* 'good opinion, reputation'. Masc: Eudoxio.

Eufemia *eu* 'good' + *phenai* 'speech'. Dim: Femia. Masc: Eufemio.

Eufrasia The origin and meaning of this name are not known. Dims: Frasia, Frecha, Pacha. Masc: Eufrasio.

Eugenia Greek *eugenes* 'well-born, noble'. Santa Eugenia was a 3rd century martyr saint. Feast December 25. Dims: Cenia, Genia, Gena, Geni, Gina, Queña. Masc: Eugenio. English: Eugenia.

Eulalia Greek *eu* 'good' + *lalios* 'speech'. Santa Eulalia, who lived in Spain in the 4th century, is patron saint of Barcelona, sailors and runaways. Feast February 12. Dims: Baia, Eula, Eulia, Lala, Lali, Laya, Olalla, Olaya, Ula. Masc: Eulalio. English: Eulalia.

Eulogia Greek *eu* 'good' + *logos* 'thought'. Dims: Locha, Lola. Masc: Eulogio.

Eunice Greek *eu* 'good' + *nike* 'victory'. In the Bible, the mother of Timothy.

Eusebia The name of the Greek goddess of piety. Dim: Cheba. Masc: Eusebio.

Eustaquia, Eustasia, Eustacia Greek *eu* 'good' + *stakhys* 'sword'. These are feminine forms of the name of the patron saint of Madrid, Eustaquio.

Eva, Eve Hebrew for 'life'. In the Bible, the wife of Adam. Dim: Evita. Masc: Evelio. English: Eve, Eva.

Evangelina Greek *euangelion* 'good news'. Dims: Eva, Evina. Masc: Evangelino. English: Evangeline.

Evarista Greek *eu* 'good' + *aristos* 'best, noblest'. Masc: Evaristo.

Evelina see Aveline

Evina A diminutive of Evangelina.

Evita A diminutive of Eva made famous by Eva Peron, 20th century president's wife and later president of Argentina.

Exaltación Spanish for 'exaltation'. A Christian name, referring to La Exaltación de la Santa Cruz (the Exaltation of the Holy Cross) miraculously immovable from the Holy Land. Feast September 14. Dim: Salto.

Ezti Basque for 'honey'.

Fabia, Favia From the Roman family name Fabius, derived from Latin *faba* 'bean'. Dim: Fabi. Masc: Fabio.

Fabiana, Faviana From Fabianus, a Roman name meaning 'a relative of Fabius', derived from Latin *faba* 'bean'. Dim: Fabi. Masc: Fabián, Fabiano.

Fabiola, Faviola A Late Latin diminutive of Fabia. The Italian Santa Fabiola founded the first Western hospital in the 4th century. Feast March 21.

Fabricia, Fabrizia From a Roman clan name, Fabricius, derived from Latin *fabrica* 'arts and crafts'. Dim: Bricia. Masc: Fabricio.

Fabriciana From Fabricianus, a Roman name meaning 'a relative of Fabricius', derived from Latin *fabrica* 'arts and crafts'. Masc: Fabriciano.

Facha A diminutive of Bonifacia.

Facunda Latin *facundia* 'eloquence'. Masc: Facundo.

Fana, Fani Diminutives of Estefanía.

Fanny A diminutive of Francisca.

Fara Feminine of Faro. Also a diminutive of Burgundófara, a medieval name.

Fata A diminutive of Fausta.

Fátima An Arab name, borne by the daughter of the prophet Muhammad. In Spanish-speaking countries, the name is usually bestowed in honor of Nuestra Señora del Rosario de Fátima (Our Lady of Fatima), patroness of Portugal. Feast May 13.

Fausta, Faustina Latin *fausta* 'lucky, favorable'. Dim: Fata. Masc: Fausto, Faustino.

Favia see Fabia

Faviana see Fabiana

Faviola see Fabiola

Fe Spanish for 'faith'. Santa Fe is patron saint of pilgrims and soldiers. Feast August 1. English: Faith.

Febe, Febes Greek *phoibos* 'bright, pure', an epithet of Artemis, Greek goddess of hunting and the moon. The name was mentioned in the New Testament by Saint Paul. English: Phoebe.

Federica Germanic *fridu* 'peace' + *ric* 'king'. Masc: Federico. English: Frederica.

Fedra In Greek myth, this was the name of the daughter of King Minos of Crete. English: Phaedra.

Fefe A diminutive of Josefa and Josefina.

Fela A diminutive of Rafaela.

Felia A diminutive of Ofelia.

Felicia see Felisa

Feliciana Latin *felix* 'fortunate, lucky'. Dim: Chana. Masc: Feliciano

Felicidad Spanish for 'happiness, prosperity, success'. Catalan: Felicitat. English: Felicity.

Felicita, Felícitas Latin *felix* 'lucky, fortunate'. Dim: Chita. English: Felicity.

Felina This name may be from Latin *felis* 'cat' or *felix* 'fortunate, lucky'.

Felipa, Filipa Greek *philein* 'to love' + *hippos* 'horses' = 'one who loves horses'. Diminutive: Lipa. Masc: Felipe. English: Philippa.

Felisa, Felicia Latin *felix* 'lucky, fortunate. Dim: Zita. Masc: Félix. English: Felicia.

Felma A diminutive of Filomena.

Femia A diminutive of Eufemia.

Fermina Latin *firmus* 'strong, firm'. Dim: Mina. This name is popular in the Philippines. Masc: Fermín.

Fernanda, Ferdinanda Germanic *fridu* 'peace' + *nand* 'ready, prepared'. Dims: Fernandina, Nanda. Catalan: Ferranda. Masc: Ferdinando, Fernán, Fernando.

Fidelia, Fidela Latin *fidelis* 'faithful, honest'. Dim: Lela. Masc: Fidel, Fidelio.

Fidelina Latin *fidelis* 'faithful, honest'. Dim: Lina. Masc: Fidelino.

Fifi A diminutive of Josefina and Sofía.

Filis, Phylis Greek *phyllis* 'leaves, leafy branch'. A nymph in Greek myth, and a favorite name of ancient Greek and Roman poets. It became popular again during the Renaissance. English: Phyllis.

Filomena, Filomela Greek *philos* 'friend' + *menos* 'strength'. Dims: Felma, Mela, Mena. Masc: Filemón, Filomeno. English: Philomena.

Fina A diminutive of names ending in '-fina', such as Serafina and Josefina, and also used as a name in its own right.

Fita A diminutive of Sofía.

Flavia From the Roman clan name, Flavius, derived from Latin *flavus* 'yellow'. Masc: Flavio.

Flaviana From a Roman name, Flavianus 'a relative of Flavius'. Masc: Flaviano.

Flor, Flores Spanish for 'flower, flowers'. Dim: Florita.

Flora Latin *flos, floris* 'flower'. Flora was the Roman goddess of flowers and of spring. Dim: Flori. Masc: Floro. English: Flora.

Florencia Latin *florens* 'flowering'. Masc: Florencio. English: Florence.

Florentina Latin *Florentinus* 'a native of Florence'. Masc: Florentino.

Flores see Flor

Floriana Latin *flos, floris* 'flower'. Masc: Florián, Floriano.

Florida Latin *floridus* 'flowery'. Masc: Florido.

Florina, Florinia Latin *flos, floris* 'flower'. Masc: Florino, Florinio.

Florinda A blend of Flora and Linda.

Fontsanta see Fuensanta.

Fortuna Latin *fortuna* 'luck, chance'. Fortuna Dea was the Roman goddess of good fortune. Dim: Tina. Masc: Fortuno.

Fortunata Latin *fortunatus* 'fortunate, lucky'. Masc: Fortunato.

Franca Germanic *franc* 'a Frank'. The Franks, a Germanic-speaking tribe, invaded the western Roman Empire in the 5th century. Masc: Franco.

Francisca, Francesca Latin Francisca 'a Frankish woman'. Dims: Chicha, Fanny, Franca, Frasquela, Frasquita, Paca, Pancha, Paquita, Quita. Masc: Francisco. English: Francesca.

Frasia, Frecha Diminutives of Eufrasia.

Frasquita A diminutive of Francisca.

Freda, Frida Originally diminutives of Alfreda and other names containing the Germanic name-element *fridu* 'peace'.

Fuencisla Nuestra Señora de Fuencisla is patroness of Segovia, Spain. Feast the last Sunday of September.

Fuensanta Spanish *fuente* 'fountain' + *santa* 'holy'. Nuestra Señora de Fuensanta is the patroness of Murcia, Spain. Feast September 9. Dim: Fuenta. Catalan: Fontsanta.

Fulgencia Latin *fulgentius* 'lightning'. Dim: Chencha. Masc: Fulgencio.

Fulvia From the Roman clan name Fulvius, derived from Latin *fulvus* 'yellow-brown'. Masc: Fulvio.

Gabina Latin *Gabinius* 'a native of Gabio [an ancient city near Rome]'. Dim: Gabi. Masc: Gabino.

Gabriela Feminine form of Gabriel, 'man of God' in Hebrew. Dims: Gabi, Gaby. English: Gabrielle, Gabriela.

Gail, Gaila Diminutives of Abigaíl.

Gala, Galia Germanic for 'Gauls' an early Celtic tribe of present-day France. Gala Placidia was a Visigoth queen.

Galena, Galenia Greek *galene* 'serene, calm'. Masc: Galeno.

Garbiñe, Garabina Basque forms of Inmaculada.

Gaspara Feminine of Gaspar, a name of unknown origin, perhaps Persian, attributed by medieval tradition to one of the three Magi who carried gifts to the Christ Child.

Gema, Gemma Latin *gemma* 'gem, precious stone'.

Gena, Genia Diminutives of Eugenia.

Genara, Jenara Latin Ianuarius, Roman god of beginnings and the new year. Masc: Genaro, Jenaró.

Genciana Latin *gentiana* 'gentian', the name of several mountain plants with blue or purple flowers. Masc: Genciano.

Generosa Latin *generosus* 'noble birth'. Masc: Generoso.

Genón, Genona Diminutives of Genoveva.

Genoveva Welsh *gwen* 'shining, holy' + *hywfar* phantom, spirit', the same source as Guinivere. Santa Genoveva (Saint Genevieve) is patron saint of Paris. Her prayers were said to have halted Atilla the Hun. Feast January 3. Dims: Genón, Genona, Geva, Veva. Catalan: Ginebra. English: Genevieve, Jenifer.

Gentzane Basque form of Paz.

Georgia, Georgina Greek *ge* 'earth' + *ergon* 'work' = 'one who works the earth, a farmer'. Dim: Gina. Masc: Jorge. English: Georgia, Georgina. See also Jorgina.

Geraldina Germanic *gar* 'spear' + *wald* 'ruler, governor'. Dim: Dina. Masc: Geraldo. English: Geraldine.

Gerarda, Gerardina Germanic *gar* 'spear' + *hard* 'strong, brave'. Masc: Gerardo.

Germana Latin *germana* 'sister'. Santa Germana is the patron saint of shepherdesses. Feast June 15. Masc: Germán, Germano. English: Germaine.

Gerónima see Jerónima

Gertrudes, Gertrudis, Gertrudia Germanic *gar* 'spear' + *drudi* 'strength'. Santa Gertrudis (Saint Gertrude the Great) was a 13th century mystic and writer. Feast November 17. Dims: Gertina, Tulia. English: Gertrude.

Gervasia From the French name Gervais, derived from Germanic *gar* 'spear'. Masc: Gervasio, Gervaso.

Gessami A Catalan form of Jazmín and Yazmín.

Gesuina A diminutive of Jesusa.

Geva A diminutive of Genoveva.

Gidita A diminutive of Brígida.

Gigi A diminutive of Gisela.

Gilberta Germanic *gisil* 'pledge' + *berht* 'shining, brilliant'. Dims: Beta, Gila. Masc: Gilberto.

Gilda Once a diminutive of Hermenegilda, later a name in its own right. Dim: Gildi. English: Gilda.

Gina Originally a diminutive of Regina, Eugenia, Georgina and Jorgina, and now a name in its own right.

Ginebra Catalan form of Genoveva.

Ginesa Latin *genus* 'origin'. Masc: Ginés.

Ginia A diminutive of Virginia.

Gisela, Isela Germanic *gisil* 'pledge'. Dims: Gigi, Gisel. English: Giselle.

Gladis, Gladys Welsh *gwlad* 'nation, sovereignty'.

Gloria Spanish for 'glory, fame'. Dims: Glori, Goya. English: Gloria.

Gloriana A blend of Gloria and Ana.

Gorri, Gure, Guria Basque *gorri* 'red'.

Goya A diminutive of Gloria.

Gracia Spanish for 'grace'. This name can signify the personal qualities of grace and charm or Divine Grace, represented by the Virgin Mary as Nuestra Señora de Gracia (Our Lady of Grace). Feast September 8. Gracia is also a diminutive of Altagracia and Engracia. English: Grace.

Graciana, Agraciana Blends of Gracia and Ana.

Gracias Spanish for 'thanks'.

Graciela Latin diminutive of Gracia. Dims: Chela, Cheya.

Gracilia, Graciliana Latin *gracilis* 'thin'. Masc: Graciliano.

Graciosa Spanish for 'gracious'.

Gregoria Greek *gregorios* 'watchful, vigilant'. Masc: Gregorio.

Greta A diminutive of Margarita.

Griselda, Gricelda Germanic *gris* 'grey' + *hild* 'battle'. A name made popular in the tales of Chaucer and Boccacio. Dims: Chela, Grisel, Selda, Zelda.

Guadalupe A blended name, from Arabic *wadi* 'river' + Latin *lupus* 'wolf'. There are two sanctuaries of the Virgin Mary by this name. The older, in Cáceres, Spain, was established by San Leandro. Feast September 8. Another is in Mexico, where the Virgin appeared in 1531. Our Lady of Guadalupe is the patroness of Mexico and the Americas. Feast December 12. Dims: Guada, Lupe, Pita, Lupina, Lupita.

Guillerma, Guillermina, Willemina Germanic *wil* 'will' + *helm* 'protector'. Dims: Guilla, Ilma, Mina, Nina, Vilma. Masc: Guillermo, Guillermino.

Guiomar, Guiomara, Xiomara Germanic *wit* 'wide' + *mar* 'fame'.

Gundelina, Gundelinda Welsh *gwenn* 'shining' + *dolen* 'link'. A name made popular by tales of King Arthur. English: Gwendolyn.

Gure, Guria see Gorri

Gurutzi, Guruzne Basque forms of Cruz.

Gustava Norse *Gautr*, a tribal name + *stafr* 'staff'. Masc: Gustavo.

Haidée, Haydée, Aidée, Heidi These similar names come from two different literary sources. The English poet Lord Byron used the name in his poem, *Don Juan*. The Swiss writer, Johanna Spyri, named the heroine of her 1881 children's book Heidi, a Swiss German diminutive of Adelheid (a cognate of the Spanish name Adelaida).

Halima Arabic 'calm, peaceful'.

Harmodia, Harmonia, Armonia Greek *harmodios* 'agreable, harmonious'. Masc: Harmodio, Harmonio.

Heidi see Haidee

Heladia see Hélida

Helena see Elena

Helga, Elga, Olga German *heilige* 'holy'.

Heliana see Eliana

Hélida, Hélidia, Élida, Élidia, Alida, Alidia Greek Hellas 'a Greek person'. Masc: Hélido, Heladio.

Heloísa see Eloísa

Henriqua see Enriqua

Hermelinda, Herlinda, Ermelinda, Erlinda Germanic *ermin* 'entirely' + *lind* 'sweet, pleasing'. Diminutives: Mela, Meli. Masc: Ermelando.

Hermenegilda Germanic *ermin* 'whole, entire' + *hild* 'combat'. Dim: Gilda, Hermila. Masc: Hermenegildo.

Herminia, Erminia, Ermina Names derived from Germanic *ermin* 'whole, entire'. Dims: Hermita, Mimi, Mina, Nina. Masc: Herminio, Erminio.

Hermosa Spanish for 'beautiful'.

Hernanda A variant of Fernanda. Dims: Nanda, Nanon. Masc: Hernando.

Hersilia, Hersila, Ercilia, Ercila, Ersilia, Ersila The name of a legendary Sabine woman who was carried off by Romulus, founder of Rome. The meaning of the name is unknown. Dim: Chila.

Higinia Greek *higinos* 'vigorous'. Dim: Ginia. Masc: Higinio.

Hilaria Latin *hilaris* 'cheerful'. Dims: Hilari, Lala. Masc: Hilario, Hilaro. English: Hilary, Hillary.

Hilda, Ilda Originally diminutives of women's names ending in '-ilde', from Germanic *hild* 'combat'. English: Hilda.

Hipólita Greek *hippos* 'horses' + *lytos* 'free, stampeding'. The name of the legendary queen of the Amazons. Dims: Poli, Polita. Masc: Hipólito.

Honesta Latin *honestus* 'honored, respectable'. Masc: Honesto.

Honorata Latin *honoratus* 'honored'. Masc: Honorato.

Honoria, Honora, Onora, Onoria Latin *honor* 'honor'. Dim: Nora.

Hortensia, Ortensia From the Roman clan name Hortensius, derived from Latin *hors, hortis* 'flower'. Dims: Tencha, Chencha. English: Hortense.

Iara, Yara 'Woman' in the native Tupi language of South America.

Icía Galician form of Cecilia.

Ida From the name of the mountain in Italy which was in ancient times the home of the cult of the goddess Cybele. English: Ida.

Idalena, Idalina Blends of Ida and Elena or Elina.

Idoya, Idoi, Idurre 'Pool, fountain' in Basque, and the name of a sanctuary of the Virgin Mary. Feast the Monday after Pentecost.

Ignacia Latin *ignata* 'burning, ardent'. Dim: Nacha. Masc: Ignacio.

Ilaria see Hilaria

Ilda see Hilda

Ileana, Iliana Rumanian forms of Elena.

Ilma A diminutive of Guillerma.

Ilona The origin of this name is not certain It might be a variant of Elena or Ileana.

Imaculada see Inmaculada

Imelda Germanic *ermin* 'entirely' + *hild* 'battle'. Dim: Mela.

Ina Originally a diminutive of women's names ending in '-ina'.

Indalecias Feminine form of Indalecio, from Basque *inda* 'strength'.

Inés, Inéz, Ynés, Ynéz, Agnese Greek *hagne* 'pure'. Santa Inés, who died as a child martyr in around 300 AD, is the patron saint of young girls. Feast January 21. Dims: Inesita, Nechi, Sita, Yaecita. Catalan: Agnés. Basque: Añes. English: Inez.

Inmaculada, Imaculada Spanish for 'immaculate'. A name given in honor of La Inmaculada Concepción de la Virgen María, the Immaculate Conception of the Virgin Mary. Feast December 8. Dim: Inma.

Inocencia, Inocenta, Inocentia From Latin *innocens* 'blameless'. Diminutives: Cenci, Chenchi, Inza. Masc: Inocencio, Inocente.

Iolanda Catalan form of Yolanda.

Iosune Basque form of Jesusa.

Iracema 'Honey' in the native Tupi language of South America.

Irene, Irenia, Irenea Greek *Eirene* 'peace', name of a Greek goddess of peace. Dims: Nea, Renica, Reniquita. Basque: Ireñe. Masc: Ireneo, Irenio. English: Irene.

Iris Greek for 'rainbow'. In Greek myth, Iris was messenger of the gods. Feast of the Virgin of Arco Iris September 4.

Irma, Erma Originally diminutives of names beginning with Germanic *ermin* 'whole, entire', later names in their own right. Dims: Ermina, Irmina. English: Irma.

Irune Basque form of Trinidad.

Isa A diminutive of Elisa and Isabela.

Isabel, Isabela, Isabella Spanish forms of Elizabeth, a Biblical name meaning 'God gives' in Hebrew. This name originated in the Provence region of France and from there it spread to Spain, where it became extremely popular, and was the name of the famous queen who supported the voyages of Columbus. Feast July 4. Dims: Bel, Bela, Belica, Belicia, Bella, Belita, Chaba, Chabel, Chabela, Isa, Isabelina, Sabel, Sabela, Yssa, Yza. Masc: Isabelo. English: Isabel.

Isaura Latin for 'native of Isauria [a province in Asia]'. Masc: Isauro.

Isela see Gisela

Isidora, Isadora Greek Isis, a goddess + *doron* 'gift' = 'a gift of the goddess Isis'. Masc: Isidoro, Isadoro. English: Isadora.

Isidra, Ysidra From the same source as Isidora (above). Masc: Isidro, Ysidro.

Isolda Celtic *adsiltia* 'she who is gazed at'. The heroine of the medieval legend, *Tristan and Isolde*. Dims: Chole, Isolina.

Itatí 'White stone' in the native Guarani language of South America. Nuestra Señora de Itatí is venerated at a shrine near Buenos Aires, Argentina.

Itxaro Basque form of Esperanza.

Itxaso Basque 'sea, ocean'. A name bestowed in honor of the Virgin as Nuestra Señora del Mar (Our Lady of the Sea).

Itziar Basque 'star', the equivalent of the Spanish names Estela and Estrella.

Ivana Slavic form of Juana.

Ivet, Iveta From Catalan variants of the French name, Yvette, derived from Germanic *iv* 'yew wood'.

Izarne, Izarra Basque forms of Estela.

Jacinta, Jacinda Greek *hyakinthos* 'a dark lily'. Dim: Chinta, Cinta, Cinda. Masc: Jacinto.

Jacoba Feminine form of Jacob, from Hebrew 'heel-grabber' or 'supplanter'. It was said that the biblical Jacob held onto his twin brother Esau's heel as he was born. Dim: Jacobina.

Jacquelina, Jaquelina These are Spanish forms of the French name Jacqueline (feminine form of Jacques). In Spanish, they are used as feminine forms of Jaime.

Jaione Basque form of Natividad.

Jamila, Yamila Arabic 'beautiful'.

Jana, Janina Catalan forms of Juana.

Jasone Feminine form of Jason, from Iason, a Greek form of Joshua, a Hebrew name meaning 'God is salvation'.

Javiera see Xaviera

Jazmín, Jazmina, Yasmín, Yasmina From the Persian word for the flower, jasmine. Catalan: Gessami.

Jenara see Genara

Jerónima, Gerónima From Greek *hieros* 'holy' + *onoma* 'name'. Masc: Jerónimo, Gerónimo.

Jesica, Jessica Feminine form of Jesé, which means 'he beholds' in Hebrew. Dim: Jesi. English: Jessica.

Jesús The Aramaic form of the Hebrew name Joshua 'God is salvation'. Given to girls as a middle name, 'de Jesús'.

Jesusa Feminine form of Jesús, which is the Aramaic form of Joshua, meaning 'God is salvation' in Hebrew. Diminutives: Chita, Chucha, Chuchita, Chusita, Chuyita, Gesuina. Basque: Iosune.

Jimena, Jimenia, Ximena Feminine forms of Jimeno, which is a variant form of Simeón.

Joana Catalan form of Juana.

Joaquina 'God will build' in Hebrew. Dims: China, Quina. Catalan: Joaquima. Galician: Xaquina. Masc: Joaquín.

Joelda Feminine form of Joel, from the Hebrew 'God is lord'.

Jone Basque form of Juana.

Jordana Feminine form of Jordan, from Hebrew 'flowing downward'.

Jorgelina, Jorgina Feminine forms of Jorge, from Greek *georgos* 'farmer'. Dim: Gina. Masc: Jorge. English: Georgina.

Josefa Feminine form of José, 'God makes great' in Hebrew. Dims: Chebita, Chefa, Chepa, Chofa, Fefe, Fina, Pepa, Pepina, Pepita, Sefa. Catalan: Josepa. Basque: Yosebe. English: Josepha.

Josefina A Spanish variant of the French name Josephine. Dims: Fefe, Fifi, Fina, Pepa, Pepina. English: Josephine.

Jovana, Jovanna From an Italian name, Giovanna.

Jovita From Iovis, name of the Roman sky god.

Juana Feminine of Juan, from Hebrew 'God is gracious'. Diminutives: Janina, Juaneta, Juanita, Juanisha, Nita. Catalan: Joana. Basque: Jone. Galician: Xohana. English: Joan, Johanna.

Juanita This popular name originated as a diminutive of Juana.

Judit, Judita, Yudit Hebrew 'a Jewish woman' or 'woman from Judea'. An Old Testament name, popular in Catalunya. Dims: Judy, Yudi. English: Judith, Judy.

Julia From the Roman first name Iulia. The meaning of the name is not known. Dim: Julita. Masc: Julio. English: Julia.

Juliana, Julina From the Roman name Iuliana 'relative of Iulius'. Dim: Liana. Basque: Julene. Masc: Juliano, Julián. English: Juliana, Julianna.

Julieta The Spanish version of an Italian name, Giulietta. It became popular as the name of the heroine of Shakespeare's play, *Romeo and Juliet*. English: Juliet.

Justa Latin *iustus* 'just, righteous'. Santa Justa, a 3rd century martyr, is patroness of Seville, Spain, and of potters. Feast July 19. Masc: Justo.

Justina, Justiana From the Roman clan name Iustinus, derived from Latin *iustus* 'just, righteous'. Dims: Justia, Tina. Masc: Justino. English: Justine.

Justiniana From the Roman name, Iustinianus, derived from Latin *iustus* 'just, righteous'. Masc: Justiniano.

Juvencia Latin *iuventius* 'youth'. Masc: Juvencio

Juventina From the Roman clan name Iuventinus, derived from Latin *iuventus* 'youth'. Masc: Juventino.

K Officially, there is no such letter in Spanish (there is in Basque). Parents sometimes substitute 'k' for 'c' in girls' names such as Karla and Erika.

Karen, Kari, Karina see Carina

Karmele, Karmel Basque forms of Carmel and Carmen.

Katalin, Katarin, Katixa Basque forms of Catalina, Catarina.

Kati, Katina, Katixa Diminutives of Catalina and Catarina.

Kauldi Basque form of Claudia.

Koikile Basque form of Cecilia.

Kontxexi Basque form of Concepción.

Kristiñe Basque form of Cristina.

La Reina, Lareina 'Queen' in Spanish. These names are bestowed in honor of the Virgin Mary as Queen of Heaven. Feast of Santa María Reina August 22.

Ladislada Slavic *volod* 'government' + *slav* 'glory'. Masc: Ladislao.

Laia, Laya Catalan diminutives of Eulalia.

Laida, Layda Diminutives of Adelaida.

Lala A diminutive of Adela, Eulalia and Hilaria.

Lali, Lalia Diminutives of Eulalia.

Lana A diminutive of Antoliana.

Landa A diminutive of Yolanda.

Landra A diminutive of Alandra.

Lara, Larisa From a Spanish Royal surname derived from a place name in Burgos. Its meaning is not known.

Laura Latin *laurus* 'laurel tree', emblem of victory in ancient Greece and Rome. Santa Laura was a 9th century abbess of Cordoba, Spain. Feast October 19. Masc: Lauro. English: Laura.

Laureana Latin *laureatus* 'crowned by laurels, victorious'. Masc: Laureano.

Laurencia A feminine form of Laurencio, an early form of Lorenzo.

Laurentina From the Roman clan name Laurentius, derived from Latin *laurus* 'laurel'. Masc: Laurentino.

Laurinda Latin *laurus* 'laurel', signifying victory + a Germanic name-element *lind* 'sweet'. Masc: Laurindo.

Lavinia, Lavina In the ancient Roman epic, the *Aeneid*, Lavinia was the wife of Aeneas, the founder of Rome. The origin of the name is not known.

Laya A dim. of Adelaida and Eulalia.

Lázara The feminine form of Lázaro, which means 'God, my help' in Hebrew.

Léa see Lía

Leala see Leila

Leandra Feminine form of Leandro, from Greek *leon* 'lion' + *andros* 'man'. In Greek legend, Leander would swim the treacherous Hellespont every night to visit Hero, his beloved. Leandra is also a diminutive of Alejandra.

Leila, Leala Persian 'night'. This name was popularized in the 19th century by the English writer, Lord Byron.

Leire see Leyre

Lela A diminutive of Adela.

Lelia From a Roman clan name, Laelius. Its meaning is not known. Dim: Lelica. Masc: Lelio.

Lena, Leni Diminutives of girls' names ending in '-lena', such as Elena and Magdalena.

Leocadia Greek Leukadia, the name of an island in the Ionian Sea. Santa Leocadia, a 3rd century martyr, is the patron saint of Tolédo, Spain. Feast December 9. Catalan: Llogàia. Masc: Leocadio.

Leona Greek *leon* 'lion'. Masc: León. English: Leona.

Leonarda Germanic *liut* 'people' + *hard* 'strong, brave'. Masc: Leonardo.

Leoncia Greek *leonteios* 'like a lion'. Masc: Leoncio.

Leonila, Leonela From a French medieval diminutive of León (derived from Latin *leo* 'lion'). Masc: Leonilo.

Leonor, Leonora These were originally diminutives of Eleonor and Eleonora and later became names in their own right. Dims: Leoni, Nora. English: Lenore.

Leopolda, Leopoldina Germanic *liut* 'people' + *bald* 'bold, brave'. Dims: Pola, Polda. Masc: Leopoldo.

Letanía Spanish for 'litany'. This Marian name refers to recitation of the rosary.

Leticia, Letizia Latin *laetitia* 'joy'. Dims: Leti, Licha, Ticha. English: Letitia.

Levina Hebrew 'joined'. Masc: Levi.

Lexi A diminutive of Alejandra.

Leyre A name bestowed in honor of Nuestra Señora de Leyre, who is venerated at the monastery of San Salvador in Leyre, Spain. Feast August 15.

Lía, Léa 'Cow' in Hebrew. Along with Rachel, Leah was one of the two matriarchs of Israel. Lía is also a diminutive of Amalia. English: Leah.

Liana A diminutive of Juliana, and also a blended name, from Lía and Ana.

Liberata, Librada Latin *libero* 'to liberate [from sin]'. This is a name from early Christian times. Diminutive: Libra. Masc: Liberato, Liberado.

Libertad Spanish for 'liberty'. A name bestowed upon a child to express a political ideal.

Licha A diminutive of Alicia, Elisabet, and Leticia.

Licia Latin *Lycia*, a region in southwest Turkey. The name of the region comes from Greek *lukos* 'wolf'. Licia is also a diminutive of Alicia.

Lidia, Lydia Latin *Lydia*, a region in western Turkey. The name derives from Ludos, name of the legendary ancestor of the Lydian people. English: Lydia.

Lidón see Lledó

Ligaya, Ligia Greek *lygios* 'adaptable', or perhaps *lygys* 'melodious'. Ligia is also a diminutive of Eligia.

Lila A diminutive of Emilia and Dalila

Lili, Lilí Diminutives of Alicia, Carmelita, Liliana and Lilia.

Lilia, Lila Latin *lilium* 'lily'. A white lily, symbolizing purity, is the flower of the Virgin Mary. Two other Spanish names, Susana and Azucena, also mean lily. Dim: Lili. English: Lily, Lila.

Liliana, Lilián Blends of Lilia and Ana. Dim: Lili. English: Lilian, Lillian.

Liliosa A blend of Lilia and Rosa.

Lilit Sumerian for 'night demon, screech owl, the goddess of storms'. According to Jewish tradition, Lilith was Adam's first wife. English: Lilith.

Lina Greek *linus* 'flax'. Flax was an important plant in ancient times, providing both linen cloth and oil. Lina is also a diminutive of names ending in '-lina', including Adelina, Avelina, Catalina and Paulina. Masc: Lino.

Linares This Marian name is bestowed in honor of Nuestra Señora de Linares, venerated at a sanctuary in Córdoba, Spain. Feast first Sunday in May.

Linda Spanish for 'pretty'. Linda is also a diminutive of names ending in '-linda', such a Belinda and Ermelinda.

Lipa A diminutive of Felipa.

Lira, Liria Greek *lyra* 'lyre [a stringed instrument]'.

Lisa A diminutive of names containing 'lisa', such as Belisa, Elisabet and Melisa.

Lisandra From Greek *lysandros* 'liberator'. Masc: Lisandro.

Liseta From the French Lisette, a diminutive of Elisabet.

Lita Greek *litos* 'simple, easy'. Masc: Lito. Lita is also a diminutive of names ending in '-la' and '-lita', such as Manuela and Carmelita.

Livia A diminutive of Olivia.

Livia, Livina From the Roman family name Livius, which is derived from Latin *lividus* 'bluish'.

Lledó, Lidón Spanish for 'hackberry tree'. A name for the Virgin Mary as Nuestra Señora del Lledó, patroness of Castellón de la Plana, Spain. Feast first Saturday in May.

Llogàia Catalan form of Leocadia.

Llúcia Catalan form of Lucía. Llúcia is patron saint of Mallorca, Spain.

Locha, Lochi Diminutives of Eloísa and Eulogia.

Lodia A diminutive of Elodia.

Lola, Lolo Originally diminutives of Dolores, Carlota, Eulogia, Lorenza and other names containing 'lo'. Lola is now a name in its own right. Dims: Loleta, Lolita.

Lolicia A blend of Lola and Alicia.

Lolita see Lola

Loña, Loni Diminutives of Apolonia.

Lora, Lore Diminutives of Dolores, Lorena, Lorenza, Loreto and Lourdes.

Lore Basque for flower.

Lorena From Lorraine, the name of a region in eastern France where an apparition of the Virgin Mary was seen. Feast May 30. Dim: Lora, Lore, Loren. English: Lorraine.

Lorenza Latin *Laurens,* 'native of Laurentium', a port city south of Rome that was named for the laurel trees that grew there. Dims: Enza, Lola. Masc: Lorenzo.

Lores A diminutive of Dolores.

Loreto, Loreta Latin *lauretum* 'place of laurels'. Our Lady of Loreto is associated with a shrine in Loreto, Italy, which is said to be the house in Nazareth where the Virgin Mary was born. According to legend, the house was transported to Italy either by supernatural forces, or by crusaders. Feast December 10. Catalan: Lloret, Lloreto. Basque: Lorete.

Lota, Loti Diminutives of Carlota.

Lourdes, Lordes Basque 'craggy slope'. In 1858, Lourdes, near the Pau River in the French Pyrenees, was the site of an apparition of the Virgin Mary. Feast

February 11. Dims: Lulu, Milú, Lourde-cita. Basque: Lorda.

Luanna A blended name, from Luisa or Lucía and Ana.

Luca A diminutive of Lucrecia.

Luce Basque form of Lucía.

Lucelia Latin diminutive of Lucía, from *lux, lucis* 'light'.

Lucero Latin *lucifer* 'light-bringer', also a name for the morning star.

Lucha A diminutive of Luz.

Lucía A Roman first name, from Latin *lux, lucis* 'light'. Santa Lucía, a 4th century martyr, was a very popular saint during the Middle Ages. Feast December 13. Dims: Lu, Luci, Lucita, Lucy. Catalan: Llúcia. Basque: Luce. Masc: Lucio. English: Lucy.

Luciana From a Roman name, Lucianus 'a relative of Lucius', derived from Latin *lux, lucis* 'light'. Dims: Luci, Lucie, Chana. Masc: Luciano.

Lucila, Lucilia, Lucilla From Lucilla, a diminutive of the Roman name, Lucia, derived from Latin *lux, lucis* 'light'. English: Lucille.

Lucina Latin *lux, lucis* 'light'. An epithet of the Roman goddesses Juno and Diana, who presided at childbirth, drawing newborns into the light.

Lucinda A blend of Lucía and Linda.

Lucrecia, Lucrece Latin *lucror* 'to gain, to win'. Dims: Luca, Quecha.

Luella A blend of Luisa and Ella.

Luisa, Aloisa Germanic *hlod* 'glorious' + *wig* 'combat'. Santa Luisa of Marillac (1591-1660) is the patron saint of social workers. Feast March 15. Dims: Luisina,

Lula, Lulita, Lulu. Masc: Luis. English: Louisa, Louise.

Luján This Marian name is given in honor of the Virgin Mary as Nuestra Señora de Luján, who is venerated at a sanctuary near Buenos Aires, Argentina. Feast May 8.

Lula A diminutive of Luisa, Luz and Obdula.

Lulu A diminutive of Lourdes and Luisa.

Luminosa Latin *luminosa* 'brilliant'.

Luna Spanish for 'moon'.

Lupa, Lupe Latin *lupus* 'wolf'. Masc: Lobo, Lope, Lupo.

Lupina, Lupita Dims. of Guadalupe.

Luz Spanish for 'light'. This name is bestowed in honor of the Virgin Mary as Nuestra Señora de la Luz (Our Lady of Light). Feast July 1. Dims: Chita, Lucecita, Lucha, Lula.

Luzdivina A blend of Luz and Divina.

Luzmaría A blend of Luz and María.

Lya see Lía

Lydia see Lidia

Mabel From Old French *amabel* 'lovely'.

Mabél A blend of María and Isabel.

Macarena Greek *makaros* 'lucky, fortunate'. The name of a neighborhood in Seville, Spain, location of a shrine of the Virgin as Nuestra Señora de la Esperanza. Dim: Maca.

Macaria Greek *makaros* 'fortunate'. Masc: Macario.

Maciela see Marisela

Mada, Madena, Madina Diminutives of Magdalena.

Madelón Catalan form of Magdalena.

Madona, Madonna Italian *ma donna* 'my lady', a title of the Virgin Mary. A newly popular baby name.

Magalí Catalan form of Margarita.

Magdalena, Magdalen, Madalena From a New Testament name, María de Magdala (Mary Magdalen). Magdala is a place in Galilee. Feast July 22. Dims: Elena, Lena, Mada, Madena, Madina, Magda, Maida, Malena, Nena. Catalan: Magalí, Madelón. Basque: Matxalen, Maialen. Masc: Magdaleno. English: Madeleine, Madeline.

Magina Latin *magnus* 'great'. Masc: Magín.

Maia see Amaya, Maya and María

Maica Short form of María del Carmen.

Maida A diminutive of Magdalena.

Maite A blend of María and Teresa.

Maite, Maitana, Maitane 'Beloved' in Basque, a name used as the equivalent of the Spanish name, Encarnación. Feast March 25.

Malén 'Maiden' in the native Araucanian language of Chile and Argentina.

Malena A blend of María and Elena, and also a diminutive of Magdalena.

Malina see Melina

Malinda see Melinda

Malisa A blend of the names María and Elisa.

Malva, Malvina, Melva Malva is a Spanish word for 'daisy'. Dims: Mal, Malvi. English: Malvina.

Manda, Mandy Diminutives of Amanda and Armanda.

Manoli, Manola see Manuela

Manón A French diminutive of Marie.

Manuela, Manoela 'God is with us' in Hebrew. Dims: Manola, Manoli, Mela, Melita, Neli, Nelia. Masc: Manuel.

Mar Spanish for 'sea, ocean'. As Nuestra Señora del Mar (Our Lady of the Sea), the Virgin Mary is patroness of sailors and of Almería and Santander, Spain. Feast September 15. Basque: Itxaso.

Mara 'Bitterness' in Hebrew, from the name of a place near the Red Sea, a site of pools of bitter water. Mara is also a diminutive of Dámaris.

Maravillas, Maravilla 'Miracles, miracle' in Spanish. These names are given in honor of the Virgin Mary as Nuestra Señora de las Maravillas (Our Lady of Miracles). Feast September 10. Catalan: Maravella.

Marcela, Marcelia From a Roman family name Marcellus, a diminutive of Marcus, from name of the Roman war god, Mars. Dims: Chela, Marquita. Masc: Marcelo. English: Marcella.

Marcelina From Marcellinus, a Roman name meaning 'a relative of Marcellus'. Dims: Chela, Lina. Masc: Marcelino.

Marcia From Marcius, a Roman clan name derived from the name of the god of war, Mars. Dims: Chicha, Marcina, Marcita. Masc: Marcio. English: Marcia, Marsha.

Marciana From Marcianus, a Roman name meaning 'a relative of Marcius'. Masc: Marciano.

Maren Basque form of Mariana.

Marga, Margie, Margo Diminutives of Margarita.

Margarita Latin *margarita* 'pearl', from the Greek, and probably derived from a Persian word meaning 'child of light'. Saint Margaret of Antioch, a martyr of the 3rd century, was said to have slain a dragon. Feast July 20. Dims: Greta, Magi, Marga, Margie, Margo, Marguita, Rita. Catalan: Magalí, Margarida. Basque: Margarete. Masc: Margarito. English: Margaret.

Mari A Basque form of María. Also the name of a preChristian Basque goddess.

María From Miriam, a Hebrew name of uncertain meaning, perhaps 'bitter' or 'grieved' or 'rebellion'. The name of the mother of Jesus was considered too holy to be the name of a person before the Middle Ages. Feasts January 1, August 15. Natividad de María September 8. Dims: Mari, Marica, Marieta, Marietta, Marita, Moya. Basque: Miren, Mari. English: Mary, Maria.

Mariam see Miriam

Mariana, Marián, Marién A name signifying devotion to the Virgin Mary. An Ecuadorian saint, Mariana de Jesús de Quito (1618-1645), whose prayers halted an earthquake, is remembered May 26. Basque: Maren. Masc: Mariano. English: Marian.

Marianela A blend of María and Estela, Isabela or another '-ela' name.

Mariángeles A shortened form of María de los Ángeles.

Mariazel From the name of a 10th century shrine of the Virgin Mary in Austria. Feast September 15.

Maribe, Maribel A blend of María and Isabel.

Marica A diminutive of María.

Maricelia, Maricel Blends of María and Celia.

Maricruz A blend of María and Cruz.

Mariel, Mariela Blends of María and Isabel or Isabela.

Marién see Maríana

Mariesa, Marisa A blend of María and Teresa or Elisa.

Marieta A diminutive of María.

Marifé A blend of María and Fe.

Marilena, Marlena Blends of María and Elena.

Marilú A blend of María and Luisa.

Mariluz A blend of María and Luz.

Marimar A shortened form of María del Mar.

Marina A diminutive of María and also a feminine form of Marino, from Latin *marinus* 'of the sea'.

Marinés A blend of María and Inés.

Marión, Mariona Catalan variants of Maríana.

Maripepa A blend of María and Josefa.

Mariquel A blend of María and Raquel.

Mariquen A blend of María and Enrica.

Mariquita A blend of María and Chiquita.

Marisel, Marisela Blends of María and Gisela.

Marisela see also Marcelia

Marisidra A blend of María and Isidra.

Marisol A blend of María and Sol.

Maristela A blend of María and Estela.

Marita A diminutive of María.

Maritxu, Mirentxu Basque diminutives of María.

Marquesa A feminine form of Marcos.

Marquita A diminutive of Marcela.

Marta 'Woman, mistress of the house' in Aramaic. Santa Marta (Saint Martha) is patron saint of innkeepers and cooks. Feast July 29. Dim: Martita, Matty. English: Martha.

Martana A blend of Marta and Ana.

Martina From the Latin name Martinus, after the Roman god of war, Mars. Dims: Marti, Tina. Masc: Martín. English: Martina.

Martiniana From Martinianus 'a relative of Martinus' (see Martina, above). Masc: Martiniano.

Maruxa Catalan form of María.

Matea Feminine form of Mateo, which means 'gift of God' in Hebrew.

Matilde, Matilda Germanic *maht* 'force' + *hild* 'combat'. Dims: Mati, Mota, Tila, Tilda, Tilde. English: Matilda.

Matxalen Basque form of Magdalena.

Maura, Mora, Morisa, Morissa Latin *maurus* 'a Moor, a person from Northern Africa'. Masc: Mauro. English: Maura.

Mauricia From a Roman name, Mauritius, derived from Latin *maurus* 'a Moor, a person from North Africa'. Masculine: Mauricio.

Maximina, Maximiana From Roman names meaning 'a relative of Maximus', derived from Latin *maximus* 'most, best'. Dim: Maxi. Masc: Maximino.

Maya Greek *Maia* 'mother'. This Greek goddess was adopted by the Romans, who named the month of May after her.

Maya is also a diminutive of Amalia. See Amaya.

Meca A diminutive of América.

Mecha A diminutive of Mercedes and Nemesia.

Mela, Meli Diminutives of Amelia, Filomela, Manuela, Melania and Pamela.

Melania Greek *melas* 'black'. The name of two 5th century Roman saints, grandmother and granddaughter. Dims: Mel, Mela, Melani, Milena. Masc: Melanio. English: Melanie.

Melchora Feminine form of Melchor, from Persian *melk* 'king' + *quart* 'city'. In medieval popular tradition, Melchor (Melchior in English) was the name of one of the three Magi who carried gifts to the Christ Child.

Melia A diminutive of Camelia.

Melina, Mélida, Melinda Latin *mellina* 'sweet as honey'. Dim: Mela, Meli.

Melisa, Melissa Greek *melissa* 'a bee'. This name was made popular by Italian Renaissance poets. Dims: Melita, Mili, Lisa. English: Melissa.

Melisenda, Elisenda Germanic *amal* 'work' + *sind* 'path', via the Old French name Melisende. In medieval legends, the name of a daughter of Charlemagne. English: Millicent.

Mena A diminutive of Filomena.

Mencia A diminutive of Clemencia.

Mercedes Spanish for 'rewards'. Given in honor of the Virgin Mary as Nuestra Señora de las Mercedes (Our Lady of Ransom). Feasts August 10 and September 24. Dims: Chelo, Mecha, Merce, Mercedita, Merche. Catalan: Mercè.

Meritxell Virgin of a sanctuary in Andorra and patroness of that principality. Feast September 8.

Meté A diminutive of Mercedes.

Meya A diminutive of Amelia.

Mia A diminutive of Mireia, Mireya.

Micaela, Miguela Hebrew 'who is like God?' Diminutives: Caela, Caila, Mimi, Miqui, Quela. Masc: Miguel. English: Michaela.

Micha A diminutive of Artemisa.

Miche A diminutive of Mercedes.

Mila A diminutive of Camelia, Camila, Emilia, Emiliana and Milagros.

Milagros Spanish for 'miracles'. A name bestowed in honor of the Virgin Mary as Nuestra Señora de los Milagros (Our Lady of Miracles). Feast July 9. Dims: Mila, Milagritos, Mili. Catalan: Miracle. Basque: Alazne.

Milagrosa Spanish for 'miraculous'. This name is bestowed in honor of the Virgin Mary as Nuestra Señora de la Medalla Milagrosa (Our Lady of the Miraculous Medal). Feast November 27. Dim: Mila. Catalan: Miraculosa.

Milena A diminutive of Magdalena.

Mili A diminutive of Camila, Emilia, Melisa and Milagros

Milva, Milvia Latin *milvus* 'kite' (the bird).

Mimi A diminutive of Emilia, María, Miriam, Micaela and other 'm' names.

Mina A diminutive of names ending in '-mina', such as Benjamina, Carmina, Fermina and Guillermina.

Minda A diminutive of Arminda.

Minerva Latin *mens* 'mind'. Minerva was the Roman goddess of wisdom and the patroness of all the arts and sciences.

Miqui A diminutive of Micaela.

Mira Greek *myron* 'myrrh'. Masc: Miro. English: Mira, Mirra. Also a diminutive of Miranda.

Miracle Catalan form of Milagros.

Miranda Latin *miranda* 'admiring'. A name popularized by Shakespeare in his play, *The Tempest*. Dims: Mira, Randa, Randi. English: Miranda.

Mireia, Mireya Latin *mirare* 'to look at'. A popular name in Catalunya. Dim: Mia.

Miren A Basque form of María.

Miriam, Mariam, Myriam This Old Testament name could mean 'bitter' or 'grieved' or 'rebellion'. Miriam, the sister of Moses, was a prophetess. Dim: Mimi. English: Miriam.

Miroslava Slavic *meri* 'great' + *slav* 'glorious'.

Mirta An epithet of the Greek goddess of love, Aphrodite, from Greek *myrtos* 'myrtle', a tree that was sacred to her.

Misericordia Latin for 'compassion, pity, mercy'. Dims: Còia (Catalan), Cori.

Modesta Latin *modesta* 'modest'. Dim: Mota. Masc: Modesto.

Mona A diminutive of Ramona, Mónica and Simona.

Monceo, Monces Dims. of Montserrat.

Mónica Greek *monos* 'solitary, a person who lives alone'. The 4th century Santa Mónica, the mother of Saint Augustine, is patron saint of mothers. Feast August 27. Dims: Mona, Moncha. Basque: Monike. English: Monica.

Monseís A diminutive of Montserrat.

Monserrat see Montserrat.

Montaña Spanish for 'mountain'. This name is bestowed in honor of the Virgin Mary as Nuestra Señora de la Montaña. Masc: Montano.

Montserrat, Monserrat Spanish *monte aserrado* 'a saw-toothed mountain'. Nuestra Señora de Montserrat ('Mare de Déu de Montserrat' in Catalan) is represented by a Black Madonna in a shrine near Barcelona, Spain. According to legend, the statue was carved by Saint Luke and carried to Spain by Saint Peter. Nuestra Señora de Montserrat is patroness of Catalunya. Feast April 27. Dims: Monceo, Monces, Monseís, Monsita, Montse, Montsita.

Mora, Morisa, Morissa see Maura

Mota A diminutive of Modesta and Matilde.

Moya A diminutive of María.

Munira Arabic 'brilliant, shining'.

Nacha A diminutive of Atanasia and Ignacia.

Nadal Catalán form of Natividad.

Nadia The Spanish form of Nadya, a Russian name from *nadezhda* 'hope'. Dims: Nadina and Nadenia, from Nadine, a French diminutive of Nadya.

Naida A diminutive of Zenaida.

Nana A diminutive of Ana.

Nanda A diminutive of Fernanda, and Ferdinanda.

Naomi see Noemí

Narcisa Greek Narkissos, from *narkor* 'to put to sleep'. In myth, Narcissus was a young man who fell in love with his own reflection. Also the name of a flower, the narcissus. Dims: Cisa, Chicha. Masc: Narciso.

Natalena Blend of Natalia and Elena.

Natalia Latin *Natalis* 'Christmas'. Natalia de Córdoba, a Spanish saint, gave aid to early Christian martyrs. Feast July 27. Dims: Lena, Natacha, Natalena, Natalina, Natasha, Nati, Tali, Talia. Masc: Natal, Natalio. English: Natalie, Natalia.

Natividad Spanish for 'birth'. La Natividad de María (the birthday of the Virgin Mary) is celebrated September 8. Dim: Nati. Catalan: Nativitat, Nadal. Basque: Jaione.

Nazaret Spanish for the biblical city of Nazareth. A name in honor of the Virgin Mary as Nuestra Señora de Nazaret.

Nazaria Hebrew 'set apart, consecrated'. Masc: Nazar, Nazario, Názaro.

Nea A diminutive of Irene.

Nechi A diminutive of Inés.

Nekane Basque *neke* 'sorrow'. Used as the equivalent of Dolores.

Nelda A diminutive of Reinelda.

Neli A diminutive of Manuela.

Nelia A diminutive of Cornelia.

Nélida A diminutive of Cornelia, Elena and Reinalda.

Nemesia From the name of a Greek goddess of justice, Nemesis, who punished pride and arrogance. Dim: Mecha. Masc: Nemesio.

Nena, Niña Spanish for 'a baby, a little girl'. Feast of Santa Nena December 15.

Nerea, Neria From Nereus, the Greek god of the sea. Masc: Nereo.

Nereida Greek *nereid* 'sea nymph', from *Nereis* 'daughter of Nereus'.

Nerina As name invented by the Roman poet Virgil, perhaps based on the Greek word for 'sea nymph', *nereid*. Dim: Neri.

Neus Catalan form of Nieves.

Nicanora Greek *nike* 'victory' + *aner* 'man'. Dim: Nicara. Masc: Nicanor.

Nicolasa Greco-Latin *nike* 'victory' + *laus* 'praise'. Diminutives: Colasa, Nica, Nicola, Nicolina. Masc: Nicolás, Nicolau. Coleta (the Spanish version of the French name Colette) is also used. English: Nicole.

Nidia, Nydia Latin *nitidus* 'brilliant'.

Nieves Spanish for 'snows'. This name is given in honor of Nuestra Señora de las Nieves (Our Lady of the Snows), Virgin of the Basilica of Saint Mary Major in the Vatican. It is said that a miraculous snowfall occurred on the summer day in the year 435 when the basilica was dedicated. Feast August 5. Catalan: Neus. Basque: Edurne.

Nilda, Nilde Originally a diminutive of names ending in '-nilda' such as Brunilda and Leonilda.

Nina Originally a diminutive of names ending in '-nina', now a name in its own right.

Niña see Nena

Ninfa Spanish for 'nymph'. In Greek myth, nymphs were magical creatures inhabiting rivers, trees and mountains.

Nita A diminutive of Juanita and other names ending in '-na' and '-nita'.

Noelia, Noela From Noel, French for Christmas and the equivalent of Spanish Navidad. See also Natalia. Feast December 25. Masc: Noel, Noelino.

Noemí, Naomi 'My pleasantness' in Hebrew. In the Bible, Naomi was the mother-in-law of Ruth. English: Naomi.

Nola A diminutive of Arnolda.

Nona Latin *nonus* 'ninth'.

Nora Originally this was a diminutive of names ending in '-nor' and '-nora', such as Eleonor, Honora and Leonora. English: Nora.

Norma This name derives from either Latin *norma* 'rule, pattern' or Germanic *nord* 'north' + *man* 'man'. The name was popularized by the 1831 opera, *Norma,* by Vincenzo Bellini. Masc: Normán, Normando. English: Norma.

Nubia Latin name of an ancient kingdom in northeast Africa.

Nuncia Latin *nuntio* 'to announce'. Also a diminutive of Anunciación and Anunciata. Masc: Nuncio.

Núria, Nuriya "Brilliant, shining' in Arabic. The Virgin is venerated at an 11th century shrine by this name in Girona, Spain. A popular name in Catalunya. Feast September 8. Dim: Nuri.

Obdula From Abdallah, an Arabic name meaning 'he who lessens pains'. Santa Obdula was a martyr saint of Tolédo, Spain. Feast September 5. Dim: Lula.

Octavia From Octavius, a distinguished Roman family name derived from Latin *octavus* 'eighth'. Dim: Tavia. Masc: Octavio. English: Octavia.

Odila, Odilia Germanic *odo* 'wealth'. Dims: Tila, Tilia. Masc: Odilón.

Ofelia Greek *ophelos* 'aid, help'. A name made popular by William Shakespeare, who gave this name to the heroine of *Hamlet*. Dim: Felia. English: Ophelia.

Oita Catalan form of Esperanza.

Olaya, Olalla see Eulalia, Laia.

Olga see Helga

Oliana, Oriana Feminine forms of Olián, a medieval version of Julián. This name became popular during the Middle Ages —Oliana was the name of the heroine of *Amadís de Gaula,* a Spanish romance of chivalry,

Olimpia Greek Olympos, the name of the site of the Olympic games and also of the mountain home of the Greek gods. Santa Olimpia was the mother of Alexander the Great. Feast April 15. Masc: Olimpio. English: Olympia.

Olinda Germanic *lind* 'sweet, pleasing'. Masc: Olindo.

Oliva, Olivia Latin *oliva* 'olive tree'. Dim: Livia. English: Olivia.

Omara A feminine form of Omar, an Arabic name mentioned in the Bible. It means 'talkative' in Hebrew.

Ondina A water-dwelling pagan deity, somewhat like a mermaid. From Latin *unda* 'a wave'.

Onora, Onoria see Honor

Ora A diminutive of Aurora, Orora and other 'ora' names.

Oralia, Orelia see Aurelia

Oria A diminutive of Oriana. Also see Aurea.

Oriana see Oliana

Orora see Aurora

Orquídea Spanish for 'orchid'.

Osane Basque form of Remedios.

Otavia see Octavia

Otilia, Otilde Germanic *othal* 'fatherland'. Dim: Tila. Masc: Otilio.

Pabla Latin *paulus* 'small'. Feminine form of Pablo, along with Paula, Paola and Pablita.

Pablita Originally a diminutive of Pabla, later a name in its own right.

Paca, Paquita Diminutives of Francisca.

Pace A diminutive of Patricia.

Pacha A diminutive of Eufrasia.

Paciencia Latin *patientia* 'patience'. Masc: Paciente. English: Patience.

Palmira, Palmir, Palma From Latin *palma* 'palm tree'. Originally this was a name for a person who brought back a palm leaf from the Holy Land. Masc: Palmiro.

Paloma Spanish for 'a dove'. A name given in honor of the Virgin Mary as Nuestra Señora de la Paloma (Our Lady of the Dove). Feast August 15. Catalan: Coloma. Basque: Usoa. Galician: Pomba.

Pamela A name invented by the English poet Sir Philip Sydney in the 16th century. Dims: Mela, Pam, Pami.

Paquita A diminutive of Francisca.

Pascua, Pascualina, Pasquala Latin *paschalis* 'relating to Easter', from the Hebrew *pesach* 'passover'. Masc: Pascual, Pascal.

Pastora Latin *pastor* 'shepherd'. A Christian name, referring to the Virgin Mary as la Divina Pastora (the Divine Shepherdess). Masc: Pastor.

Patricia Latin *patricia* 'a noblewoman'. Dims: Pace, Pati, Patti, Tricia. Masc: Patricio. English: Patricia.

Paula, Paola, Pola Latin *paulus* 'small'. Dim: Pauleta. Masc: Paulo. English: Paula.

Paulina From the Roman name Paulinus 'a relative of Paulus'. Dims: Pauli, Lina. Masc: Paulino. English: Pauline.

Paz Spanish for 'peace'. A name given in honor of Virgin Mary as Nuestra Señora de Paz (Our Lady of Peace), patroness of El Salvador. Feast January 24. Basque: Gentzane.

Penélope In the ancient Greek epic, the *Odyssey,* this was the name of the wife of the hero Odysseus. *Penelops,* Greek for 'a duck', may be the source of this name. Dims: Pene, Peni. English: Penelope.

Pensita A diminutive of Prudencia.

Pepa, Pepita Diminutives of Josefa.

Pera A diminutive of Esperanza.

Perfecta Spanish for 'perfect'. Masc: Perfecto.

Perla Spanish for 'pearl'.

Petra Latin *petrus* 'stone'. Masc: Pedro.

Petronila, Petronela Latin diminutive of Petronius, a Roman family name derived from *petra* 'stone'. Santa Petronila was said to have been the daughter of Saint Peter. Feast March 16. Dims: Petra, Pirucha.

Phylis see Filis

Pía Latin *pia* 'pious'. Masc: Pío.

Piedad Spanish for 'pity, compassion', a name given in honor of the Virgin Mary as Nuestra Señora de Piedad (Our Lady of Piety). Feast November 21.

Pilar Spanish for 'pillar'. As Nuestra Señora del Pilar (Our Lady of the Pillar), the Virgin Mary is patroness of Zaragoza, Spain. According to tradition, the Virgin Mary appeared there, above a pillar, to Santiago. Feast October 12. Dims: Pili, Pilucha, Piluchi. Basque: Arroin.

Pina From an apparition of the Virgin Mary in the Canary Islands. Nuestra Señora del Pino is patroness of the city of Las Palmas. Also a diminutive of names ending in '-pina'.

Pirucha A diminutive of Petronila.

Pita A diminutive of Guadalupe and Agapita.

Plácida, Placidia Latin *placidus* 'quiet, gentle'. Dims: Placi, Plaza. Masc: Plácido.

Pola A form of Paula, and a diminutive of Amapola, Apolonia and Apolinaria.

Pola, Polda Diminutives of Leopolda.

Poli, Polita Diminutives of Hipólita.

Ponciana From the Roman name Pontianus 'relative of Pontius'. Dim: Chana. Masc: Ponciano.

Porcia, Portia From the Roman name Porcius, derived from Latin *porcus* 'pig'. A name made famous by the heroine of Shakespeare's *Merchant of Venice.*

Preciosa Spanish for 'precious', signifying la Preciosa Sangre de Nuestro Señor Jesucristo (the Precious Blood of Our Lord, Jesus Christ). Feast Good Friday.

Presentación Spanish for 'presentation'. See Purificación.

Prima, Primeira Latin *prima* 'first, foremost'. A name given to a first-born child. Masc: Primo.

Primavera Spanish for 'springtime'.

Priscila, Priscilla Latin diminutive of Prisca, from *priscus* 'ancient, venerable'. Dims: Cilla, Pris. Masc: Priscilo. English: Priscilla.

Prudencia Latin *prudentia* 'knowledge, especially knowledge of the future'. Dim: Pensita. Masc: Prudencio, Prudente. English: Prudence.

Puebla Spanish for 'village, people'.

Pura Spanish *pura* 'pure'. Also a diminutive of Purificación.

Pureza Spanish for 'purity'. A name bestowed in honor of the Virgin Mary as La Virgen de la Pureza (the Virgin of Purity). Feast October 16.

Purificación Spanish for 'purification'. A name bestowed in honor of Mary's purification in the temple forty days after the birth of Jesus. The official form of this name is now Presentación. Feast February 2. Dim: Chon, Pura, Puri.

Purisima Spanish for 'immaculate conception'. Feast December 8. Dim: Puri.

Quecha A diminutive of Lucrecia.

Quela A diminutive of Micaela, Raquel.

Queña A diminutive of Eugenia.

Querida Spanish for 'dear, beloved'.

Queta A diminutive of Enriqueta and Enrica.

Quilina A diminutive of Tranquilina.

Quina A diminutive of Almaquina and Joaquina.

Quinta From Quintus, a Roman name which means 'fifth, fifth child' in Latin. Masc: Quinto.

Quintina From the Roman name Quintinus 'a relative of Quintius', from Latin *quintius* 'fifth'. Originally a name for a fifth daughter. Masc: Quintín.

Quirina From Latin Quirinus, an epithet of Romulus, the legendary founder of Rome. Derived from the Sabine word *quiris* 'spear'. Masc: Quirino.

Quita A diminutive of names ending in '-ca', such as Blanca and Francisca.

Rafaela Feminine form of Rafael, 'God has healed' in Hebrew. Dim: Fela, Rafa. English: Rafaela.

Raimunda Germanic *rad* 'counsel, advice' + *mund* 'protector' (the same source as Ramona). Masculine: Raimundo.

Rainelda Germanic *rad* 'counsel, advice' + *wald* 'ruler, governor'. Dims: Raina, Raine. Also see Reinalda.

Ramira Germanic *rad* 'counsel, advice' + *miru* 'protector'. Masc: Ramiro.

Ramona Germanic *rad* 'counsel, advice' + *mund* 'protector'. Dim: Mona. Masc: Ramón. English: Ramona.

Randa, Randi Diminutives of Miranda.

Raquel Hebrew for 'ewe'. In the Old Testament, Rachel was the wife of David and mother of Joseph. Dim: Quela. English: Rachel, Raquel.

Rayén 'Flower' in the native Araucanian language of the Mapuche of Chile and Argentina.

Rebeca, Rebecca An Aramaic name from the Old Testament, the meaning of which is not known. In the Bible, the mother of Jacob and Esau. Dim: Bequi. English: Rebecca.

Refugio, Refugia Spanish for 'refuge'. A name bestowed in honor of the Virgin as Nuestra Señora de Refugio (Our Lady of

Refuge). Feast August 13. Dims: Cuca, Fucho. Masc: Refugio.

Regina Latin *regina* 'queen', signifying the Virgin Mary as Queen of Heaven, *Regina Caeli*. Feast September 7. Dim: Gina. Masc: Regis. English: Regina.

Reies see Reyes

Reina Spanish for 'queen'. A name bestowed in honor of Nuestra Señora Reina de la Paz (Our Lady Queen of Peace). Feast July 9. Also see La Reina, Lareina and Regina.

Reinalda, Rainelda, Renalda, Rinalda Germanic *rad* 'counsel, advice' + *wald* 'ruler, governor'. Dims: Nelda, Nélida, Nilda. Masc: Reinaldo, Raineldo, Rinaldo, Renaldo.

Reis Catalan form of Reyes.

Remedios Spanish *remedio* 'a remedy, a cure'. A name given in honor of the Virgin Mary as Nuestra Señora de los Remedios (Our Lady of Remedies) in her role as one who relieves suffering. She is the patroness of Alicante, Spain. Feast second Sunday in October. Catalan: Remei. Basque: Osane.

Renata Latin *renata* 'reborn'. Masc: Renato. English: Renata.

Renica, Reniquita Diminutives of Irene.

Reyes, Reies From *reyes,* Spanish for 'kings', a name bestowed in honor of the three kings who carried gifts to the Christ Child. This name may be given to a girl or a boy. La Adoración de los Reyes (the Feast of the Epiphany), is celebrated January 6. Dim: Regita. Catalan: Reis.

Ricarda, Ricaria Germanic *ric* 'king' + *hard* 'strong, brave'. Dims: Rica, Riquia. Masc: Ricardo, Ricario.

Rigoberta Germanic *ric* 'king' + *berht* 'shining, brilliant'. Dims: Berta, Riga. Masc: Rigoberto.

Rina A diminutive of Ceferina.

Riqueta A diminutive of Enrica and Enriqueta.

Riquia A diminutive of Ricarda.

Rita Originally a diminutive of Margarita. Santa Rita is a patron saint of desperate cases. Feast May 22. English: Rita.

Roberta Germanic *hrod* 'glorious' + *berht* 'shining, brilliant'. Dim: Berta. Masc: Roberto. English: Roberta.

Rocío Spanish for 'dew', ancient symbol of purity. Rocío is a Marian name, for a sanctuary of the Virgin Mary in Andalusia honoring her as Nuestra Señora del Rocío (Our Lady of the Dew). Feast Monday of Pentecost. Catalan: Rosada.

Rocita, Rochi Diminutives of Rosa.

Rodas This name might derive from either Germanic *hrod* 'glorious' or Greek *rhodos* 'rose'. English: Rhoda.

Rodriga Germanic *hrod* 'glorious' + *ric* 'king'. Masc: Rodrigo.

Rogelia Germanic *hrod* 'glorious' + *gar* 'spear'. Masc: Rogelio, Rogerio

Rolanda, Roldana Feminine forms of Rolando, from Germanic *hrod* 'glorious' + *land* 'earth, country'.

Romana, Romina Latin *Romana* 'a native of Rome'. Masc: Román, Roman, Romano.

Romea A name from early Christian times. It was given to a person who had made a pilgrimage to the city of Rome. Dim: Romina. Masc: Romeo. English: Roma.

Romilda, Romelia Germanic *hrod* 'fame' + *hild* 'combat'.

Romina see Romana

Roquelia Feminine form of Roque, from Germanic *hroc* 'shout'. Masc: Roque, Rocco.

Rosa Spanish and Latin for the flower, 'rose'. Many women's names of Germanic origin contain the similar-sounding *hros* 'horse', Rosalinda and Rosamunda, for example. Peruvian-born Santa Rosa de Lima (1586-1617) is a patron saint of the Americas. Feast August 23. Dims: Rocita, Rochi, Roseta, Rosi, Rosina, Rosita. English: Rose, Rosa.

Rosada Catalan form of Rocío.

Rosalba Latin *rosa* 'rose' + *alba* 'white'. Dims: Chaba, Rosel.

Rosalena A blend of Rosa and Elena.

Rosalía Latin *Rosalias,* a festival in which roses were placed upon the tombs of the dead. Dims: Chala, Chali, Lía. Masc: Rosalío. English: Rosalie.

Rosalina A blend of Rosa and Catalina. Dims: Chalina, Roslin.

Rosalinda, Rosinda Germanic *hros* 'a horse' + *lind* 'sweet, pleasing'. A popular name in the Middle Ages. Masc: Rosalindo, Rosalino. English: Rosalind.

Rosamaría A blend of Rosa and María. English: Rosemarie.

Rosamunda Germanic *hros* 'a horse' + *mund* 'protector'.

Rosana A blend of Rosa and Ana.

Rosario Spanish for 'rosary'. Nuestra Señora del Rosario (Our Lady of the Rosary) is patroness of Guatemala and of the cities of Cádiz and La Coruña, Spain.

Feast October 7. Nuestra Señora del Rosario de Chiquinquirá is the patroness of Colombia. Feast July 9. Diminutives: Chalo, Charín, Charo, Chayo, Rosa, Sario, Sarito. Catalan: Roser, Rosó. Basque: Agurtzane, Agurne.

Rosaura Germanic *hros* 'a horse' + *wald* 'ruler, governor'.

Rosenda Germanic *hrod* 'glorious' + *sind* 'path'. Dim: Chenda.

Roser, Rosó Catalan forms of Rosario.

Roslin A diminutive of Rosalina.

Roxana Greek Roxane, the name of the wife of Alexander the Great, probably derived from a Persian word meaning 'dawn'. Dim: Roxy. English: Roxanne.

Rubí, Rubía Spanish *rubí* 'ruby', the precious stone. English: Ruby.

Rufina From a Roman clan name, Rufinus, derived from Latin *rufus* 'red, ruddy'. Santa Rufina is patron saint of potters. Dim: Rufa. Masc: Rufino.

Rut, Ruth Hebrew 'companion'. In the Old Testament, Ruth was the ideal daughter-in-law. English: Ruth.

Sabel, Sabela Diminutives of Isabel and Isabela.

Sabina Latin *Sabinus* 'a Sabine [a member of an ancient tribe of Italy, rivals of the Romans]'. Masc: Sabino.

Sabrina The Celtic name for the goddess of the Severn River in England.

Sagrario Spanish for 'chapel'. Nuestra Señora del Sagrario is the patroness of Tolédo, Spain. Feast August 15. Dim: Sagra.

Sainza see Sancha

Salbadora, Salbatora see Salvadora

Salomé Hebrew 'healthy, harmonious'. There were two women by this name in the Bible, one was a follower of Jesus, the other was a cruel daughter of Herod. Basque: Xalome.

Salvadora, Salvatora, Salbadora, Salbatora From Late Latin *salvator* 'savior'. Dims: Chaba, Dora. Masc: Salvador, Salvadore, Salvatore.

Samanta Aramaic for 'she who listens'. English: Samantha.

Sancha, Sainza Latin *sancio* 'to consecrate, to make sacred'. Masc: Sancho. English: Sanchia.

Sandra, Sondra Originally diminutives of Alejandra, Alejandrina and Casandra. Dims: Sandi, Sandrita. Masc: Sandro. English: Sandra, Sondra.

Sandrina A diminutive of Alejandrina.

Sanjuana Feminine version of the saint's name, San Juan (Saint John).

Santa, Latin *sancta* 'sacred'. Dim: Santina. Masc: Santino.

Sara, Sarah 'A princess in Hebrew'. In the Old Testament, Sarah was the wife of Abraham. Dim: Sarita. English: Sara, Sarah.

Sario, Sarito Diminutives of Rosario.

Saturnina From Latin Saturnus, the Roman god of agriculture and civilization. Masc: Saturnino.

Saula Feminine form of Saúl.

Savana, Savanna, Savannah Spanish *sabana* 'a treeless plain' A popular name in the United States.

Sebastiana Greek *sebastos* 'honored'. Dims: Seba, Chana, Tiana. Masc: Sebastián, Sebastiano.

Sefa A diminutive of Josefa.

Segunda, Secundina Latin *secunda* 'second one', a name given to a second-born child. Masc: Segundo.

Selda A diminutive of Griselda.

Selena, Selina Greek Selene, goddess of the moon. English: Selena, Selina.

Selma A diminutive of Anselma.

Sena A diminutive of Zenona.

Serafina Hebrew 'Burning one, angel'. Dims: Fina, Pina. Masc: Serafín, Serafino.

Serena Latin *serena* 'serene, calm'. Santa Serena was the wife of Roman Emperor Domitian. English: Serena.

Severina Latin Severina 'a relative of Severus', from Latin *severus* 'strict, stern'. Masc: Severino.

Sidonia Latin 'a native of Sidon [a city in Phoenicia, now Lebanon]'. Masc: Sidonio. English: Sidney, Sidonia.

Sierra Spanish for 'a saw, a saw-toothed mountain range'. This is a popular name in the United States.

Silbe Basque form of Silvia.

Silde A diminutive of Casilda.

Silvana Latin *silvana* 'one who lives in the woods'. Dim: Vana. Masc: Silvano.

Silveria Latin *silva* 'woods'. Masc: Silverio.

Silvia Latin *silva* 'woods'. According to Roman legend, Rhea Silvia was the mother of Romulus, founder of Rome, and his twin brother Remus. The 6th century Santa Silvia was the mother of Saint Gregory the Great. Feast November 3. Dim: Chiva. Masc: Silvio. English: Sylvia.

Silvina Latin *silva* 'woods'. Dim: Vina. Masc: Silvino.

Simona Feminine form of Simeón and Simón, from Hebrew 'God hears me'. Dim: Mona. English: Simone.

Sinforosa Greek *symphora* 'companion'. Masc: Sinforoso.

Sira Latin *Sirius* 'a native of Syria. Masc: Siro.

Sita A diminutive of Inés.

Socorro Spanish for 'help'. A name bestowed in honor of the Virgin as Nuestra Señora del Perpetuo Socorro (Our Lady of Perpetual Help). Feast June 27. Dims: Coco, Cora, Coyo. Catalan: Socors.

Sofía Greek *sophia* 'wisdom'. Dims: Fia, Fifi, Fita, Sofi, Sofina. English: Sophia.

Sol Spanish for 'sun'. A name given in honor the Virgin of a sanctuary in Andalusia, Nuestra Señora del Sol. Feast December 3. As a second name, 'del Sol'. Basque: Eguzki.

Solana Latin *solana* 'a sunny place'. A name given in honor of San Francisco Solano (1549-1610), a missionary to Peru. The name could also be a blend of the names Sol and Ana.

Soledad Spanish for 'solitude'. A name is given in honor of the Virgin Mary as Nuestra Señora de la Soledad (Our Lady of Solitude). Feast Good Friday. Dims: Sole, Chola, Chole.

Sondra A diminutive of Alejandra.

Sonia From Sonja, a Russian cognate of Sofía.

Soraida, Soraya see Zoraida

Sotera Greek *soter* 'savior'. Masc: Sotero.

Stansa A diminutive of Constancia.

Stefania see Estefanía

Suelo A diminutive of Consuelo.

Susana Hebrew 'lily'. The name of the heroine of an apocryphal book of the Bible, *Susannah and the Elders*. Diminutives: Susa, Susan, Susi, Susina, Susu. English: Susan, Susanna.

Susú A diminutive of Úrsula.

Suyai, Suyay 'Hope' in the Quechua language of South America.

Suyapa Nuestra Señora de la Concepción de Suyapa is patroness of Honduras. She is named for the village where a small wooden carving of the Virgin was found in 1747.

Tabita, Tabitha 'A gazelle' in Aramaic. Tabitha, also called Dorcas, was a charitable woman mentioned in the Bible. English: Tabitha.

Tacha A diminutive of Anastasia.

Tacia, Taciana see Tatiana

Tali, Talia Diminutives of Natalia and Castalia.

Talia From Thalia, the Greek muse of comedy, a name derived from *thallein* 'to flower, to flourish'.

Tamara, Tamar Hebrew 'a date palm'. The name of three women in the Bible. One was an ancestress of King David. Dim: Tammy. English: Tamara.

Tancha A diminutive of Constancia.

Tania, Tanya Diminutives of Tatiana.

Tareixa Galician form of Teresa.

Tasha A diminutive of Ananstasia and Tatiana.

Tatiana, Taciana From the Roman family name Tatianus. The meaning of the name is not known. Dims: Tacia, Tania, Tanya, Tasha, Tiana.

Taucha A diminutive of Atocha.

Tavia A diminutive of Octavia.

Tea A diminutive of Aristea and Dorotea.

Techa A diminutive of Teresa

Teche A diminutive of Ester.

Tecla Santa Tecla, an early martyr saint, is patroness of Tarragona, Spain. Feast September 23.

Tela, Teli Diminutives of Estela.

Telina A diminutive of Etelvina.

Telma Germanic *helm* 'protector'. See the masculine form, Telmo, for an explanation of why this name begins with the letter 't'. Dim: Mita. English: Thelma.

Tencha A diminutive of Hortensia.

Teodolinda, Teolinda, Deolinda Germanic *theudo* 'people' + *lind* 'sweet, pleasing'. Dims: Delina, Linda.

Teodora Greek *theos* 'God' + *doron* 'gift'. Diminutives: Dora, Teo, Teodita. Masc: Teodoro. English: Theodora.

Teodosia Greek *theo* 'God' + *dosis* 'giving'. Masc: Teodosio. English: Theodosia.

Teofania Greek *theos* 'God' + *phanein* 'to appear', a name given in honor of the Feast of the Epiphany, January 6. Masc: Teofanio. English: Tiffany.

Teófila Greek *theos* 'God' + *philos* 'friend'. Masc: Teófilo.

Teresa A very popular name in Spanish-speaking countries. Its original meaning is not known. It may derive from either ancient Greek *theros* 'summer' or *thereios* 'wild animal'. Santa Teresa de Avila (1515-82) is patroness of Spain. Feast October 15. Santa Teresa de los Andes (1900-1920) was the first Chilean saint. Feast July 13. Dims: Tere, Techa, Tera, Ter. Catalan: Teres. Basque: Trexa. Masc: Tereso. English: Theresa.

Thena A diminutive of Athena.

Tiana A diminutive of Sebastiana and Tatiana.

Ticha A diminutive of Leticia.

Tila A diminutive of Odila and Domitila.

Tila, Tilda Diminutives of Clotilda.

Tilia A diminutive of Odilia.

Timotea Greek *time* 'honor' + *theos* 'God'. Dim: Timona. Masc: Timoteo.

Tina, Titina Diminutives of names ending in '-tina', such as Cristina, Celestina, Ernestina and Martina.

Tita From the Roman first name Titus, derived from *Tities,* the name of an early Roman tribe. The meaning of the name is not known. Masc: Tito.

Tola A diminutive of Bartolomea and Victoria.

Tolia A diminutive of Anatolia.

Tomasa Aramaic 'twin'. Masc: Tomás.

Tonia, Toña Diminutives of Antonia.

Toya A diminutive of Victoria.

Tranquilina Latin *tranquilla* 'tranquil'. Dim: Quilina. Masc: Tranquilino.

Transina Latin *transitus* 'passage'. An early Christian name signifying the passage to heaven. Masc: Tránsito.

Trena, Trenia Latin *trina* 'triple'. A name for a third child, or for the third of triplets.

Trexa Basque form of Teresa.

Tricia A diminutive of Patricia.

Trina A diminutive of Catarina.

Trinidad Spanish for 'Holy Trinity', a name given to both boys and girls. As a middle name, 'de la Santisima Trinidad'. Feast Sunday after Pentecost. Dim: Trine, Trineo, Trini. Catalan: Trinitat.

Tristana Feminine form of Tristán, the hero of the medieval romance of *Tristan and Isolde*. The meaning of this Celtic name is not known.

Trixi A diminutive of Beatriz.

Tulia, Tula From a Roman clan name, Tullius. Masc: Tulio. Tulia is also a diminutive of Gertrudes.

Txilar Basque 'heather'.

Ula A diminutive of Eulalia.

Ulrica Germanic *wulf* 'wolf' + *ric* 'king'. Masc: Ulrico.

Úrsula, Ursula Latin *ursula* 'little bear'. *The Legend of Saint Ursula and the 11,000 Virgins* was very popular in the Middle Ages. Santa Úrsula chose to die rather than marry the leader of the Huns. Feast October 21. Dim: Susú. English: Ursula.

Uxué Basque for 'a dove', the equivalent of Paloma. Feast of Nuestra Señora de Uxué December 31.

Valencia Latin *valens, valentis* 'strong, brave'. Masc: Valente, Valencio.

Valentina From the Roman clan name Valentinus, derived from Latin *valens, valentis* 'brave, strong'. Dims: Valina, Tina. Masc: Valentín.

Valeria From Valerius, a Roman clan name derived from Latin *valerus* 'strong, healthy'. Masc: Valerio. English: Valerie.

Valeriana From the Roman name Valerianus 'a relative of Valerius', from Latin *valerus* 'healthy, strong'. Masc: Valeriano.

Valina A diminutive of Valentina.

Vana Originally a diminutive of Silvana. Dim: Vanina.

Vanda see Wanda

Vanesa From Vanessa, a name invented by English writer Jonathan Swift (1667-1745).

Vanina A diminutive of Vana.

Velia A diminutive of Evelia.

Venerada, Veneranda From Latin *venerata* 'venerated'.

Vera Latin *verus* 'true'. Masculine: Vero. English: Vera.

Verdad Spanish for 'true'.

Verena Latin *verus* 'true'. Santa Verena was a 3rd century hermit saint of Switzerland. Feast August 1. Dim: Vera.

Verónica Greco-Latin *vera* 'true' + *eikon* 'image'. The cloth that Santa Verónica used to wipe Christ's face on the way to Calvary was said to have retained his true image. Feast February 4. Dim: Vera. English: Veronica.

Veva A diminutive of Genoveva.

Vica A diminutive of Virginia.

Vicenta Latin *vincens* 'conquering'. Masc: Vicente.

Victoria, Vitoria Latin and Spanish *victoria* 'victory, triumph'. The name of the Roman goddess of victory and also of Santa Victoria, a 4th century martyr who is patron saint of Córdoba, Spain. This is also a Marian name, for Nuestra Señora de Victoria (Our Lady of Victory). Feast

October 26. Dims: Bique, Bita, Tola, Toya, Victorina, Vicky. Masc: Víctor, Victorio. English: Victoria.

Vida Spanish for 'life'. A name for the Virgin, Nuestra Señora de Vida, venerated at a shrine in Girona, Spain. Feast September 8.

Vijes A diminutive of Eduvigis.

Vilma A diminutive of Guillerma.

Vina A diminutive of Alvina and other names ending in '-vina'.

Viola, Violeta Spanish for the flowers 'viola, violet'. Dim: Yola. Catalan: Violant.

Violante see Yolanda

Virginia From Verginius, the name of a Roman clan, derived from Latin *virgo, virginis* 'virgin'. Dims: Gina, Ginia, Vica. Masc: Virginio. English: Virginia.

Virtudes Spanish for 'virtues'.

Virucha A diminutive of Elvira.

Visitación Spanish for 'visit'. This name is bestowed in honor of la Visitación de la Virgen (the visit of the Virgin Mary to her cousin Elizabeth). Feast May 31.

Vita, Vida Latin *vita* 'lively, full of life'. Masc: Vito, Vidal.

Viviana, Vivián, Bibiana Latin *viva* 'alive'. Santa Viviana, an early Roman martyr, is patron saint of single women. Her assistance is sought for relief from headaches and hangovers. Feast December 2. Dims: Bibi, Viv. Masc: Viviano, Bibiano. Basque: Bibiñe. English: Vivian.

Wanda, Vanda This Slavic name was first used in Spain in the 19th century. Its meaning is not known. English: Wanda.

Wenceslada Czech *vienetz* 'crown' + *slava* 'glory'. Masc: Wenceslao.

Willemina see Guillerma

Xabe A diminutive of Xaviera.

Xalbadora, Xalvadora see Salvadora

Xalome Basque form of Salomé.

Xanat 'Vanilla' in the Totonac language of Central America.

Xandria Catalan diminutive of Alejandra.

Xaquina Galician variant of Joaquina.

Xaviera, Xabiera, Javiera Basque *etxe berri* 'new house'. Dim: Xabe. Masc: Xabier, Xavier, Javier.

Xenia Greek *xenia* 'hospitality'.

Xesca Catalan diminutive of Francisca.

Xiana Galician form of Juliana.

Xima Catalan diminutive of Joaquina.

Ximena A Catalan form of Jimena, and the name of the heroine of the medieval Spanish epic, *Cantar de mio Cid*.

Xiomara see Guiomar

Xita Catalan diminutive of Conchita.

Xoana, Xohana Galician forms of Juana.

Xóchitl, Xóchil A Nahuatl name meaning 'flower'. Xochiquetzal is the Aztec goddess of love and patroness of painters, weavers, embroiderers and sculptors.

Yaecita A diminutive of Inés.

Yamila see Jamila

Yara see Iara

Yazmín, Yasmina see Jazmín, Jazmina

Ynés, Ynéz see Inés

Yola A diminutive of Viola and Yolanda.

Yolanda, Iolanda Greek *iolanthe* 'violet flower'. Santa Yolanda, who was born to a noble family in Spain, renounced her

Europe. The language is known in Basque as Euskara.

blended name A name formed by combining two names or parts of two names, for example Marilena is a blend of María and Elena.

Catalan A language spoken in the northeast region of Spain (Catalunya and the Balearic Islands). Catalan, like Spanish, French and Italian, is a Romance language descended from Latin.

Celtic An ancient Indo-European language spoken by a group of people who, in around the 5th century BC, migrated from central Europe into Spain, France, England and Ireland. Celtic is also the name of a family of languages that includes modern Irish, Scottish Gaelic, Welsh and Breton.

Spanish and Latin word *rosa*, for the flower 'rose' and the Germanic word *hros*, which means 'horse'.

diminutive A form of a first name used by family and friends. Diminutives are formed by shortening a name, by altering sounds, or by adding a suffix such as Spanish *-ito* or *-ita*.

epithet A word or phrase consistently used alongside a name, for example 'the Great' in 'Alexander the Great'.

Etruscan Language of the Etruscans, a tribe of ancient Tuscany in Italy.

etymology The study of the origins and history of words.

feast day A Christian tradition, begun in the 3rd century, of honoring a saint on the same day each year, usually the anniversary of the saint's death.

privileged life to enter a convent. Feast December 17. Dims: Iola, Landa, Yo, Yoli, Yola. Violante is an older form.

Yólotl 'Heart' in the native Nahuatl language of Central America.

Yosebe Basque form of Josefa.

Ysabel see Isabel

Yssa, Yza Diminutives of Isabel.

Yudit see Judit

Zafira Greek *sappheiros* 'lapis lazuli'.

Zaida Arabic 'to grow'. Santa Zaida, a 12th century martyr, is the patron saint of Alcira, Spain. Feast June 1.

Zandra A diminutivesof Alejandra and Alejandrina.

Zanita A diminutive of Zenaida

Zelda A diminutive of Griselda

Zoé Greek *zoe* 'life'. Also used as a variant of Eva. English: Zoe.

Zona A diminutive of Zenona.

Zondra A diminutive of Alejandra.

Zoraida, Soraida 'A captivating woman' in Arabic. This name was made popular by Miguel de Cervantes in *Don Quixote*.

Zuleica 'Lovely, fair' in Arabic.

Zulema, Zulima From an Arabic word for 'peace'. Dims: Zuli, Zula, Zulma.

Zuri, Zuria, Zuriñe, Zurina Basque *zuri* 'white'.